# Contents

**TOPIC 1** Number     4

    Chapter 1    Number and language     4
    Chapter 2    Accuracy     7
    Chapter 3    Calculations and order     9
    Chapter 4    Integers, fractions, decimals and percentages     10
    Chapter 5    Further percentages     12
    Chapter 6    Ratio and proportion     15
    Chapter 7    Indices and standard form     19
    Chapter 8    Money and finance     23
    Chapter 9    Time     27
    Chapter 10 Set notation and Venn diagrams     28

**TOPIC 2** Algebra and graphs     31

    Chapter 11 Algebraic representation and manipulation     31
    Chapter 12 Algebraic indices     33
    Chapter 13 Equations     34
    Chapter 14 Sequences     42
    Chapter 15 Graphs in practical situations     44
    Chapter 16 Graphs of functions     47

**TOPIC 3** Coordinate geometry     53

    Chapter 17 Coordinates and straight line graphs     53

**TOPIC 4** Geometry     58

    Chapter 18 Geometrical vocabulary     58
    Chapter 19 Geometrical constructions and scale drawings     61
    Chapter 20 Symmetry     62
    Chapter 21 Angle properties     63

**TOPIC 5** Mensuration     67

    Chapter 22 Measures     67
    Chapter 23 Perimeter, area and volume     68

**TOPIC 6** Trigonometry     77

    Chapter 24 Bearings     77
    Chapter 25 Right-angled triangles     78

**TOPIC 7** Vectors and transformations     81

    Chapter 26 Vectors     81
    Chapter 27 Transformations     82

**TOPIC 8** Probability     85

    Chapter 28 Probability     85

**TOPIC 9** Statistics     90

    Chapter 29 Mean, median, mode and range     90
    Chapter 30 Collecting, displaying and interpreting data     91

# 1 Number and language

## Exercises 1.1–1.8

1  List all the prime numbers between 80 and 100.

.................................................................................................................................................. [2]

2  List all the factors of the following numbers:

   **a**  48 ............................................................................................................................. [2]

   **b**  200 ........................................................................................................................... [2]

3  List the prime factors of these numbers and express them as a product of prime numbers:

   **a**  25 ............................................................................................................................. [2]

   **b**  48 ............................................................................................................................. [2]

4  Find the highest common factor of the following numbers:

   **a**  51, 68, 85 ................................................................................................................. [2]

   **b**  36, 72, 108 ............................................................................................................... [2]

5  Find the lowest common multiple of the following numbers:

   **a**  8, 12, 16 ................................................................................................................... [2]

   **b**  $2^3, 4^2, 6$ ................................................................................................................... [2]

6  Write the reciprocal of these:

   **a**  $\frac{4}{5}$ ...................................................................[1]    **b**  $\frac{5}{2}$ ................................................................... [1]

## Exercises 1.9–1.12

1  State whether each of the following numbers is rational or irrational:

   **a**  2.5 ........................................................[1]    **b**  $0.1\dot{4}$ .................................................... [1]

   **c**  $\sqrt{17}$ ........................................................[1]    **d**  –0.03 .................................................... [1]

   **e**  $\sqrt{144}$ ........................................................[1]    **f**  $\sqrt{5} \times \sqrt{2}$ .................................................... [1]

   **g**  $\frac{\sqrt{16}}{\sqrt{4}}$ ........................................................[1]

WORKBOOK

Cambridge Assessment
International Education
Endorsed for learner support

# Cambridge IGCSE®

Core
# Mathematics

Ric Pimentel
Terry Wall

HODDER
EDUCATION

®IGCSE is a registered trademark

All exam-style questions and sample answers in this title were written by the authors.
In examinations, the way marks are awarded may be different.

Every effort has been made to trace all copyright holders, but if any have been inadvertently
overlooked, the Publishers will be pleased to make the necessary arrangements at the first
opportunity.

Although every effort has been made to ensure that website addresses are correct at time of going
to press, Hodder Education cannot be held responsible for the content of any website mentioned
in this book. It is sometimes possible to find a relocated web page by typing in the address of the
home page for a website in the URL window of your browser.

Hachette UK's policy is to use papers that are natural, renewable and recyclable products and made
from wood grown in sustainable forests. The logging and manufacturing processes are expected to
conform to the environmental regulations of the country of origin.

Orders: please contact Bookpoint Ltd, 130 Park Drive, Milton Park, Abingdon, Oxon OX14 4SE.
Telephone: (44) 01235 827720. Fax: (44) 01235 400401. Email education@bookpoint.co.uk
Lines are open from 9 a.m. to 5 p.m., Monday to Saturday, with a 24-hour message answering
service. You can also order through our website: www.hoddereducation.com

© Ric Pimentel and Terry Wall 2018

First published 2018 by

Hodder Education,
An Hachette UK Company
Carmelite House
50 Victoria Embankment
London EC4Y 0DZ

www.hoddereducation.com

Impression number 10 9 8 7 6 5 4 3 2 1

Year 2022 2021 2020 2019 2018

Cover photo © Maxal Tamor/Shutterstock

Typeset in India

Printed in the UK

A catalogue record for this title is available from the British Library.

ISBN: 978 1 5104 2167 7

**2 a** Draw and name three different 2D shapes where the area is likely to be a rational number. [3]

**b** On each of your shapes, write the dimensions that make the area a rational number. Do not work out the area. [3]

**3 a** Draw two different compound 2D shapes where the total area is likely to be an irrational number. [2]

*A compound shape is made up of more than one shape.*

**b** On each of your shapes, write the dimensions that make the total area an irrational number. Do not work out the area. [2]

**4** Complete the diagram and find the area of a square of side 2.3 units. [3]

Area = ................

## Exercises 1.13–1.18

Without using your calculator, work out:

**a** $\sqrt{0.04}$ ..................................................................................................................

.................................................................................................................................... [1]

**b** $\sqrt{1\frac{9}{16}}$ ..............................................................................................................

.................................................................................................................................... [2]

**c** $\sqrt[3]{-216}$ ..................................................................................................................

.................................................................................................................................... [2]

**d** $\sqrt[3]{15\frac{5}{8}}$ ............................................................................................................

.................................................................................................................................... [2]

## Exercise 1.19

**1** A hang-glider is launched from a mountainside. It climbs 850 m and then descends 1730 m before landing.

**a** How far below the launch point was the hang-glider when it landed?

.................................................................................................................................... [1]

**b** If the launch point was at 1850 m above sea level, at what height above sea level did the hang-glider land?

.................................................................................................................................... [1]

**2** A plane flying at 9200 m drops a sonar device onto the ocean floor. If the device falls a total of 11 500 m, how deep is the ocean at this point?

.................................................................................................................................... [2]

# 2 Accuracy

## Exercises 2.1–2.3

**1** Round the following numbers to the degree of accuracy shown in brackets:

**a** 47 (10) ............................................... [1]  **b** 1250 (100) ............................................... [1]

**c** 524 700 (1000) ........................................ [1]

**2** Write the following to the number of decimal places shown in brackets:

**a** 4.98 (1 d.p.) ........................................... [1]  **b** 18.04 (1 d.p.) ........................................... [1]

**c** 0.0048 (2 d.p.) ........................................ [1]

**3** Write the following to the number of significant figures shown in brackets:

**a** 15.01 (1 s.f.) .......................................... [1]  **b** 0.042 99 (2 s.f.) ........................................ [1]

**c** 3.049 01 (3 s.f.) ...................................... [1]

## Exercise 2.4

**1** Without using your calculator, estimate the answers to the following calculations:

**a** Multiply 22 by 4877  **b** Divide 7890 by 19

............................................... [1]  ............................................... [1]

**c** $\dfrac{47 \times 3.8}{18.8}$  **d** $\dfrac{\sqrt{140}}{2.2^2}$

............................................... [1]  ............................................... [2]

2 Estimate the shaded area of the shape. Do *not* work out an exact answer.

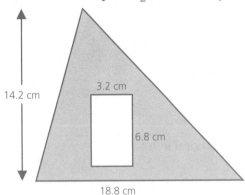

*Area of a triangle* $= \frac{1}{2}$ *base* $\times$ *height*

14.2 cm

3.2 cm

6.8 cm

18.8 cm

Estimated area = ................ [3]

## Exercise 2.5

1 Calculate the upper and lower bounds for each of the following:

   a 15 (2 s.f.) ................................................................................................ [2]

   b 12.8 (1 d.p.) ............................................................................................ [2]

   c 100.0 (1 d.p.) .......................................................................................... [2]

   d 0.75 (2 d.p.) ............................................................................................ [2]

   e 2.25 (2 d.p.) ............................................................................................ [2]

2 A town is built on a rectangular plot of land measuring 3.7 km by 5.2 km, correct to 1 d.p. What are the upper and lower limits for the length and width?

................................................................................................................ [3]

# 3 Calculations and order

## Exercises 3.1–3.4

**1** Represent the inequality $-1 \leqslant x < 4$ on the number line.

[2]

**2** Write the following sentence using inequality signs:

The finishing time ($t$ seconds) of runners in a 100 m race ranged from 12.1 seconds to 15.8 seconds.

...................................................................................................................................................[1]

**3** Write these decimals in order of magnitude, starting with the smallest:

0.5  0.055  5.005  5.500  0.505  0.550

...................................................................................................................................................[1]

## Exercises 3.5–3.8

**1** Without using your calculator, use the order of operations to work out the following:

**a** $(25 - 2) \times 10 + 4$ ................................................................................................[1]

**b** $25 - 2 \times 10 + 4$ ................................................................................................[1]

**c** $25 - 2 \times (10 + 4)$ ................................................................................................[1]

**2** Insert any brackets that are needed to make each of these calculations correct:

**a** $15 \div 3 + 2 \div 2 = 6$ ................................................................................................[1]

**b** $15 \div 3 + 2 \div 2 = 3.75$ ................................................................................................[1]

**c** $15 \div 3 + 2 \div 2 = 1.5$ ................................................................................................[1]

**3** Work out the following calculations without using your calculator:

**a** $\frac{8 + 2 \times 4}{4} - 3$ ................................................................................................[1]

**b** $-3 \times (-4 + 6) \div 4$ ................................................................................................[1]

**c** $\frac{-4 + 7 \times (-2)}{-9}$ ................................................................................................[1]

# 4 Integers, fractions, decimals and percentages

## Exercises 4.1–4.7

**1** Without using your calculator, evaluate the following:

**a** $\frac{3}{8}$ of 32 ................................................... [1]   **b** $\frac{8}{9}$ of 72 ................................................... [1]

**c** $\frac{7}{10}$ of 65 ................................................... [1]

**2** Change these mixed numbers to vulgar fractions:

**a** $6\frac{3}{5}$ ................................................... [1]   **b** $3\frac{2}{17}$ ................................................... [1]

**3** Without using your calculator, change these vulgar fractions to mixed numbers:

**a** $\frac{38}{9}$ ................................................... [1]   **b** $\frac{231}{15}$ ................................................... [1]

**4** Without using your calculator, change these fractions to decimals:

**a** $3\frac{9}{20}$ ................................................... [1]

**b** $7\frac{19}{25}$ ................................................... [1]

**c** $\frac{5}{16}$ ................................................... [2]

**5** Without using your calculator, fill in the table. Give fractions in their lowest terms.

|  | a | b | c | d | e |
|---|---|---|---|---|---|
| **Fraction** |  | $\frac{9}{20}$ |  |  | $\frac{2}{3}$ |
| **Decimal** | 0.75 |  |  | 3.08 |  |
| **Percentage** |  |  | 6.5% |  |  |

[5]

## Exercise 4.8

Work out the following using long division. Give your answers to 2 d.p.

  **a**   $4569 \div 12$

                                      **b**   $125 \div 0.13$

..................................................... [2]      ..................................................... [3]

## Exercises 4.9–4.13

**1** Without using your calculator, work out these calculations. Give answers as fractions in their simplest form.

  **a**   $3\frac{2}{5} - 1\frac{5}{6}$

.................................................................................................................. [2]

  **b**   $\frac{7}{8} - 2\frac{2}{9} + 1\frac{2}{3}$

.................................................................................................................. [3]

**2** Without using your calculator, work out these calculations. Give answers as fractions in their simplest form.

  **a**   $\frac{2}{5} \times 1\frac{2}{9}$

.................................................................................................................. [2]

  **b**   $\left(\frac{4}{9} - 1\frac{4}{5}\right) \div \frac{2}{3}$

.................................................................................................................. [3]

**3** Change these mixed numbers to decimals:

  **a**   $3\frac{4}{9}$

.................................................................................................................. [2]

  **b**   $5\frac{3}{8}$

.................................................................................................................. [2]

# 5 Further percentages

## Exercises 5.1–5.3

**1** Express the following as percentages:

   **a** 0.25 ........................................................ [1]   **b** 0.6 ........................................................... [1]

   **c** $\frac{3}{8}$ ......................................................... [1]   **d** $\frac{7}{8}$ ........................................................... [1]

**2** Work out:

   **a** 25% of 200 ................................................................................................................... [1]

   **b** 75% of 200 ................................................................................................................... [1]

   **c** 12% of 400 ................................................................................................................... [1]

   **d** 130% of $300 ............................................................................................................... [1]

   **e** 60% of $200 ................................................................................................................. [1]

   **f** 62.5% of 56 ................................................................................................................. [1]

**3** In a street of 180 houses, 90 of them have one occupant, 45 have two occupants, 36 have three occupants, and the rest have four or more occupants.

   **a** What percentage of houses has fewer than four occupants?

      ......................................................................................................................................... [2]

   **b** What percentage of houses has four or more occupants?

      ......................................................................................................................................... [1]

**4**  **i** Simplify the following fractions.

   **ii** Express them as a percentage.

     **a** $\frac{72}{90}$  **i** ........................................................................................................ [1]

           **ii** ........................................................................................................ [1]

     **b** $\frac{45}{75}$  **i** ........................................................................................................ [1]

           **ii** ........................................................................................................ [1]

     **c** $\frac{26}{39}$  **i** ........................................................................................................ [1]

           **ii** ........................................................................................................ [1]

         *Cambridge IGCSE® Core Mathematics Workbook*

**5** Three friends share $180. Ahmet gets $54, Jo gets $81 and Anna the rest. What percentage of the total amount of money does each receive?

...................................................................................................................................[3]

**6** Petrol costs 78.5 cents/litre, and 61 cents of this is tax. Calculate the percentage of the cost that is tax.

...................................................................................................................................[2]

**7** Tim buys the following items:

| | |
|---|---|
| Newspaper | 35 cents |
| Pen | $2.08 |
| Birthday card | $1.45 |
| Sweets | 35 cents |
| Five stamps | 29 cents each |

**a** If he pays with a $10 note, how much change will he get? ....................................[1]

**b** What percentage of the $10 note has he spent?

...................................................................................................................................[2]

# Exercise 5.4

**1** Increase each number by the given percentage.

**a** 180 by 25%  ..........................................................................................[1]

**b** 75 by 100%  ..........................................................................................[1]

**c** 250 by 250% ..........................................................................................[1]

**2** Decrease each number by the given percentage.

**a** 180 by 25%  ..........................................................................................[1]

**b** 150 by 30%  ..........................................................................................[1]

**c** 8 by 37.5%  ..........................................................................................[1]

**3** The value of shares in a mobile phone company rises by 135%.

**a** If the value of each share was originally 1620 cents, calculate, to the nearest dollar, the new value of each share.

.................................................................................................................................................[2]

**b** How many shares could now be bought with $10000?

.................................................................................................................................................[2]

**4** In one year, the market value of a house rose by 14%. If the value of the house was $376000 at the start of the year, calculate its new value at the end of the year.

.................................................................................................................................................[3]

**5** Unemployment figures at the end of the last quarter increased by 725000. If the increase in the number of unemployed this quarter is 7.5% fewer than the last quarter, calculate the increase in the number of people unemployed this quarter.

.................................................................................................................................................[3]

# 6 Ratio and proportion

## Exercise 6.1

**1** A bottling machine fills 3000 bottles per hour. How many can it fill in a minute?

.................................................................................................................................[1]

**2** A machine prints four sheets of A4 per minute. How many can it print in an hour?

.................................................................................................................................[1]

## Exercises 6.2–6.5

**1** 4 g of copper is mixed with 5 g of tin.

  **a** What fraction of the mixture is tin? ...................................................................[1]

  **b** How much tin is there in 1.8 kg of the same mixture? ...................................[1]

**2** 60% of students in a class are girls. The rest are boys.

  **a** What is the proportion of girls to boys, in its lowest terms?.......................[1]

  **b** What fraction of the same class are boys? ....................................................[1]

  **c** If there are 30 students in the class altogether, how many are girls? ........[1]

**3** A recipe needs 300 g of flour to make a dozen cakes. How many kilograms of flour would be needed to make 100 cakes?

.................................................................................................................................[1]

**4** 80 g of jam is needed to make five jam tarts. How much jam is needed to make two dozen tarts?

.................................................................................................................................[1]

**5** The ratio of the angles of a triangle is 1:2:3. What is the size of the smallest angle?

.................................................................................................................................[1]

**6** A metre ruler is broken into two parts in the ratio 16:9. How long is each part?

.................................................................................................................................[2]

7 A motorbike uses a petrol and oil mixture in the ratio 17:3.

   a How much of each is there in 25 litres of mixture?

   ...................................................................................................................................... [2]

   b How much petrol would be mixed with 250 ml of oil?

   ...................................................................................................................................... [2]

8 A brother and his sisters receive $2500 to be split in the ratio of their ages. The girls are 15 and 17 years old and the boy is 18 years old. How much will they each get?

   ...................................................................................................................................... [3]

9 The angles of a hexagon add up to 720° and are in the ratio 1:2:4:4:3:1. Find the size of the largest and smallest angles.

   ...................................................................................................................................... [3]

10 A company shares profits equally among 120 workers so that they get $500 each. How much would they each have got had there been 125 workers?

   ...................................................................................................................................... [3]

11 The table represents the relationship between speed and time taken for a train to travel between two stations. Complete the table.

| Speed (km/h) | 60 | | | 120 | 90 | 240 |
|---|---|---|---|---|---|---|
| Time (h) | 1.5 | 3 | 4 | | | |

[2]

**12** A shop can buy 75 shirts costing $20 each. If the price is reduced by 25%, how many more shirts could be bought?

......................................................................................................................[3]

**13** It takes 30 hours for three people to dig a trench.

   **a**  How long will it take:

     **i**  Four people .......................................................................................[1]

     **ii**  Five people? ......................................................................................[1]

   **b**  How many people would it take to dig a trench in:

     **i**  15 hours ...........................................................................................[1]

     **ii**  45 hours? ..........................................................................................[1]

**14** A train travelling at 160 km/h takes five hours to make a journey. How long would it take a train travelling at 200 km/h?

......................................................................................................................[2]

**15** A swimming pool is filled in 81 hours by three identical pumps. How much quicker would it be filled if nine similar pumps were used instead?

......................................................................................................................[3]

# Exercise 6.6

**1** A metal cube of side 3 cm has a mass of 2700 g.

   **a**  What is its density?

......................................................................................................................[2]

  **b**  What would be the mass of a similar cube of side 2.5 cm?

  ..................................................................................................................................................................[3]

**2**  The Roman city of London was built within walls which enclosed a square of side 1.6 km. Its population was 60 000. Today, London is within a rectangle 27 km by 20 km and has the same average population density. What is the current population in millions to 2 d.p.?

  ..................................................................................................................................................................[5]

**3**  The population of Earth is about 7000 million people. The surface area of Earth is 5100 million square km. The population of Australia is 24.5 million and its population density is 0.25 of that of the world population density. Calculate the approximate surface area of Australia.

  ..................................................................................................................................................................[5]

# 7 Indices and standard form

## Exercises 7.1–7.4

**1** Simplify the following using indices:

**a** $2 \times 2 \times 2 \times 3 \times 3 \times 4 \times 4 \times 4$ ................................................................................................. [1]

**b** $2 \times 2 \times 2 \times 2 \times 4 \times 4 \times 4 \times 4 \times 4 \times 5 \times 5$ ..................................................................... [1]

**c** $3 \times 3 \times 4 \times 4 \times 4 \times 5 \times 5 \times 5$ ........................................................................................... [1]

**d** $2 \times 7 \times 7 \times 7 \times 7 \times 11 \times 11$ ................................................................................................. [1]

**2** Use a calculator to work out the following:

**a** $14^2$ ............................................. [1]    **b** $3^5 \times 4^3 \times 6^3$ ...................................... [1]

**c** $7^2 \times 8^3$ ...................................... [1]    **d** $13^2 \times 2^3 \times 9^4$ .................................. [1]

**3** Simplify the following using indices:

**a** $11^5 \times 6^3 \times 6^5 \times 6^4 \times 11^2$ ................................................................................................. [1]

**b** $5^4 \times 5^7 \times 6^3 \times 6^2 \times 6^6$ ....................................................................................................... [1]

**c** $12^6 \div 12^2$ ........................................................................................................................................ [1]

**d** $13^5 \div 13^2$ ........................................................................................................................................ [1]

**4** Simplify:

**a** $(9^2)^2$ ........................................... [1]    **b** $(17^2)^5$ ........................................... [1]

**c** $(2^2)^4$ ........................................... [1]    **d** $(8^2)^3$ ........................................... [1]

**5** Simplify:

**a** $9^2 \times 5^0$ .................................... [1]    **b** $7^3 \times 7^{-2}$ .................................... [1]

**c** $16^3 \times 16^{-2} \times 16^{-2}$ ................... [1]    **d** $18^0 \div 3^2$ .................................. [2]

**6** Work out the following without using your calculator:

**a** $2^{-2}$ ................................................................................................................................................. [2]

**b** $7 \times 10^{-1}$ ....................................................................................................................................... [2]

**c** $3 \times 10^{-2}$ ....................................................................................................................................... [2]

**d** $1000 \times 10^{-3}$ ................................................................................................................................. [2]

**7** Work out the following without using your calculator:

**a** $16 \times 2^{-2}$ ...................................... [2]  **b** $128 \times 2^{-6}$ ................................... [2]

**c** $144 \times 6^{-2}$ ...................................... [2]  **d** $100\,000 \times 10^{-6}$ ............................. [2]

# Exercise 7.5

Evaluate the following without using your calculator:

**a** $49^{\frac{1}{2}}$ .................................................................................... [1]

**b** $225^{\frac{1}{2}}$ ................................................................................... [1]

**c** $125^{\frac{1}{3}}$ ................................................................................... [1]

**d** $1000\,000^{\frac{1}{3}}$ ......................................................................... [1]

**e** $343^{\frac{1}{3}}$ ................................................................................... [2]

**f** $625^{\frac{1}{4}}$ ................................................................................... [2]

**g** $81^{\frac{1}{4}}$ .................................................................................... [2]

**h** $1728^{\frac{1}{3}}$ ................................................................................. [2]

# Exercise 7.6

Work out the following without using your calculator:

**a** $\dfrac{17^0}{2^2}$ .................................................................................. [2]

**b** $\dfrac{27^{\frac{2}{3}}}{3^2}$ .................................................................................. [3]

**c** $\dfrac{64^{\frac{1}{2}}}{4^2}$ .................................................................................. [2]

**d** $\dfrac{1^0}{2^3}$ ................................................................................... [2]

**e** $\dfrac{4^{\frac{1}{2}}}{2^2}$ .................................................................................. [2]

**f** $64^{-\frac{1}{2}} \times 2^3$ ................................................................... [3]

**g** $121^{-\frac{1}{2}} \times 11^2$ ............................................................. [3]

**h** $729^{-\frac{1}{3}} \div 3^{-2}$ ............................................................................................................[3]

**i** $4^{\frac{1}{2}} \times 4^{-2} \times \frac{1}{4}$ ...................................................................................................[3]

**j** $27^{\frac{1}{3}} \times 81^{-2}$ ..........................................................................................................[3]

## Exercises 7.7–7.10

**1** Write the following numbers in standard form:

    **a** 37 000 000................................................ [1]   **b** 463 million ............................................ [1]

**2** A snail slides at an average speed of 6 cm per minute. Assuming it continues to slide at this rate, calculate how far it travels, in centimetres, in 24 hours. Write your answer in standard form.

.................................................................................................................................[2]

**3** Earth has a radius of 6400 km. A satellite 350 km above Earth follows a circular path as shown in the diagram:

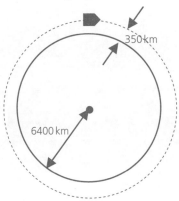

    **a** Calculate the radius of the satellite's path. Give your answer in standard form.

.................................................................................................................................[2]

    **b** Calculate the distance travelled by the satellite in one complete orbit. Give your answer in standard form correct to one decimal place.

.................................................................................................................................[3]

4 Write the following numbers in standard form:

a 0.000045 ............................................. [1]   b 0.000000000367 ....................................... [1]

5 Deduce the value of $x$ in each of the following:

a $0.03^3 = 2.7 \times 10^x$ ................................................................................................. [1]

b $0.04^x = 1.024 \times 10^{-7}$

............................................................................................................................... [2]

# 8 Money and finance

## Exercise 8.1

The table shows the exchange rate for €1 into various currencies:

| Brazil | 2.6 Brazilian reals | New Zealand | 1.5 New Zealand dollars |
|--------|---------------------|-------------|-------------------------|
| China | 8.0 Chinese yuan | Sri Lanka | 162 Sri Lanka rupees |

Convert:

a  150 Brazilian reals to euros .......................................................................................[1]

b  1000 Sri Lanka rupees to euros ...................................................................................[1]

c  500 Chinese yuan to New Zealand dollars.

.........................................................................................................................................[3]

## Exercises 8.2–8.3

1  Manuela makes different items of pottery. The table shows the amount she is paid per item and the number of each item she makes.

| Item | Amount paid per item | Number made |
|------|----------------------|-------------|
| Cup | $2.30 | 15 |
| Saucer | $0.75 | 15 |
| Teapot | $12.25 | 3 |
| Milk jug | $3.50 | 6 |

a  Calculate her gross earnings.

.........................................................................................................................................[2]

b  Tax deductions are 18% of gross earnings. Calculate her net pay.

.........................................................................................................................................[3]

**2** A caravan is priced at $9500. The supplier offers two options for customers who don't want to pay the full amount outright at the start:

Option 1: A 25% deposit followed by 24 monthly payments of $350

Option 2: 36 monthly payments of $380.

**a** Calculate the amount extra a customer would have to pay with each option.

..............................................................................................................................................[4]

**b** Explain why a customer might choose the more expensive option.

..............................................................................................................................................

..............................................................................................................................................[2]

**3** A baker spends $3.80 on ingredients per cake. If he sells each cake for $9.20, calculate his percentage profit.

..............................................................................................................................................[2]

**4** A house is bought for $240 000. After five years its value has decreased to $180 000. Calculate the average yearly percentage depreciation.

..............................................................................................................................................[3]

## Exercises 8.4–8.7

**1** What simple rate of interest is paid on a deposit of $5000 if it earns $200 interest in four years?

..............................................................................................................................................[3]

**2** How long will it take a principal of $800 to earn $112 of simple interest at 2% per year?

......................................................................................................................................[3]

## Exercises 8.8–8.10

**1** A couple borrow $140 000 to buy a house at 5% compound interest for three years. How much will they pay at the end of the three years?

......................................................................................................................................[3]

**2** A man buys a car for $50 000. He pays with a loan at 10% compound interest for three years. What did his car cost him?

......................................................................................................................................[3]

**3** Monica buys some furniture for $250 with the option of not having to pay anything back for three years. The compound interest rate on the deal is 8%. Calculate the amount Monica will have to pay back after three years.

......................................................................................................................................[3]

**4** At the beginning of the year Pedro borrows $1000. Over the next five years he doesn't borrow any more money or pay any of the original loan back, but finds that his debt has doubled. What was the compound interest charged?

......................................................................................................................................[4]

**5** A boat was bought for $6000. After three years its value halved. What was the percentage loss in compound terms?

..................................................................................................................................................................[4]

**6** An internet company grows by 20% each year.

**a** Explain why it will not take five years to double in size.

..................................................................................................................................................................

..................................................................................................................................................................[2]

**b** When will it double in size?

..................................................................................................................................................................[4]

## Exercise 8.11

**1** The value of a mobile phone decreases from $240 when new to $60 after three years.

**a** Calculate the percentage depreciation in the value of the phone.

..................................................................................................................................................................[2]

**b** Calculate the average yearly percentage depreciation.

..................................................................................................................................................................[1]

**2** A rare stamp was bought for $800000. 18 years later it was sold for $1.5 million. Calculate the percentage profit.

..................................................................................................................................................................[2]

**3** A camera was bought for $600. Five years later it was worth $120. Calculate the average yearly percentage depreciation in the camera's value.

..................................................................................................................................................................[3]

# 9 Time

## Exercises 9.1–9.2

**1** A cyclist sets off at 09 25 and his journey takes 327 minutes. What time does he finish cycling?

...............................................................................................................................................[2]

**2** A plane travels 7050 km at an average speed of 940 km/h. If it lands at 13 21, calculate the time it departed.

...............................................................................................................................................[3]

**3** A train travelling from Paris to Istanbul departs at 16 30 on a Wednesday. During the journey it stops at several locations. Overall, the train travels the 2280 km distance at an average speed of 18 km/h.

   **a** Calculate the time taken to travel to Istanbul.

...............................................................................................................................................[2]

   **b** What day of the week does the train arrive in Istanbul?

...............................................................................................................................................[1]

   **c** What time of the day does the train arrive in Istanbul?

...............................................................................................................................................[3]

**4** A plane flies between two cities. Each flight lasts 6 hours 20 minutes. The table shows the arrival or departure times of the four daily flights. Write the missing times.

| Departure | 05 40 | | | 22 55 |
| --- | --- | --- | --- | --- |
| Arrival | | 14 35 | 21 10 | |

[4]

# 10 Set notation and Venn diagrams

## Exercise 10.1

1 {Moscow, London, Cairo, New Delhi, …}

   a Describe this set in words.

   ....................................................................................................................................... [1]

   b Write down two more elements of this set.

   ....................................................................................................................................... [2]

2 {euro, dollar, yen, …}

   a Describe this set in words.

   ....................................................................................................................................... [1]

   b Write down two more elements of this set.

   ....................................................................................................................................... [2]

3 Consider the set $P$ = {Barcelona, Real Madrid, Benfica, Ajax, Juventus}.

   Write down two more possible elements of the set.

   ....................................................................................................................................... [2]

4 Consider the set $R$ = {Beethoven, Mozart, Greig, Brahms}.

   a Describe this set in words.

   ....................................................................................................................................... [1]

   b Write down two more possible elements of this set.

   ....................................................................................................................................... [2]

## Exercises 10.2–10.3

**1** Consider the Venn diagram below:

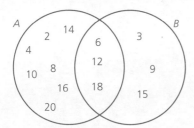

**a** Describe the elements of set *A* in words.

...............................................................................................................................................[1]

**b** Describe the elements of set *B* in words.

...............................................................................................................................................[1]

**c** Answer true or false:

**i** $A \cap B = \{6, 12, 18\}$ ........................... [1]     **ii** $A \cup B = \{6, 12, 18\}$ ..................................... [1]

**2** Sets *X* and *Y* are defined in words as follows:

$X$ = {square numbers up to 100}          $Y$ = {cube numbers up to 100}

**a** Complete the following sets by entering in the numbers:

$X = \{$.............................................................................................................................$\}$ [2]

$Y = \{$.............................................................................................................................$\}$ [2]

**b** Draw a Venn diagram showing all the elements of *X* and *Y*.

[3]

**c** Enter the elements belonging to the following set:

$X \cap Y = \{$...........................................................................................................................$\}$ [2]

**3** The sets given below represent the letters of the alphabet in each of three English cities:

$P = \{c, a, m, b, r, i, d, g, e\}$, $Q = \{b, r, i, g, h, t, o, n\}$ and $R = \{d, u, r, h, a, m\}$

   **a** Draw a Venn diagram to illustrate this information.

[3]

   **b** Complete the following statements:

      **i** $Q \cup R = \{$.........................................................................................$\}$ [1]

      **ii** $P \cap Q \cap R = \{$.............................................................................$\}$ [1]

## Exercise 10.4

A class of 15 students was asked what pets they had. Each student had either a dog ($D$), cat ($C$), fish ($F$), or a combination of them.

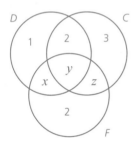

   **a** If $n(D) = 10$, $n(C) = 11$ and $n(F) = 9$, calculate:

      **i** $x$ ...........................................................................................................[3]

      **ii** $y$ ...........................................................................................................[2]

      **iii** $z$ ...........................................................................................................[1]

   **b** Calculate $n(C \cup F)$ ...................................................................................[2]

# 11 Algebraic representation and manipulation

## Exercises 11.1–11.4

**1** Expand the following and simplify where possible:

**a** $-5(x+4)$ .................................................. [1]   **b** $-3(y-2)$ .................................................. [1]

**c** $4a(2b+4)$ .................................................. [1]   **d** $6(2c-8)$ .................................................. [1]

**2** Expand the following and simplify where possible:

**a** $-3a^2(2a-3b)$ .................................................................................................... [2]

**b** $12(p+3)-12(p-1)$ .................................................................................................... [2]

**c** $5a(a+3)-5(a^2-1)$ .................................................................................................... [2]

**3** Expand the following and simplify where possible:

**a** $\frac{1}{2}(8x+4)+2(3x+6)$ ....................................................................................................

.................................................................................................... [2]

**b** $2(2x+6y)+\frac{3}{4}(4x-8y)$ ....................................................................................................

.................................................................................................... [2]

**c** $\frac{1}{8}(16x-24y)+4(x-5y)$ ....................................................................................................

.................................................................................................... [2]

**4** Expand and simplify:

**a** $4p-3(p+7)$ .................................................................................................... [1]

**b** $3q(2+7r)+2r(3+4q)$ ....................................................................................................

.................................................................................................... [2]

**c** $-2x(2y-3z)-2y(2z-2y)$ ....................................................................................................

.................................................................................................... [2]

**d** $\frac{a}{9}(27+72b)$ ....................................................................................................

.................................................................................................... [2]

**e** $\frac{p}{2}(4q-4)-\frac{p}{3}(9q-9)$ ....................................................................................................

.................................................................................................... [2]

## Exercise 11.5

Expand and simplify:

a $(a + 8)(a + 4)$ ............................................ [2]      b $(c - 9)(c - 9)$ ............................................ [2]

c $(j + k)(k - m)$ ............................................ [2]      d $(2n - 5)(3n + 4)$ ............................................ [2]

e $(1 - 4p)(2 - 3p)$ ............................................ [2]      f $(b - 3)(b + 3)$ ............................................ [2]

## Exercise 11.6

Factorise:

a $3a + 6b$ ............................................ [1]

b $-14c - 28d$ ............................................ [1]

c $42x^2 - 21xy^2$ ............................................ [2]

d $m^3 - m^2n - n^2m$ ............................................ [2]

e $-13p^2 - 32r^3$ ............................................ [2]

## Exercises 11.7–11.8

Evaluate the expressions below if $p = 3, q = -3, r = -1$ and $s = 5$.

a $p - q + r - s$ ............................................ [2]

b $5(p + q + r + s)$ ............................................ [2]

c $2p(q - r)$ ............................................ [2]

d $p^2 + q^2 + r^2 + s$ ............................................ [2]

e $-p^3 - q^3 - r^3 - s^3$ ............................................ [2]

## Exercise 11.9

Make the letter in bold the subject of the formula:

a $a\boldsymbol{b} + c = d$ ............................................ [2]

b $a\boldsymbol{b} - c = d$ ............................................ [2]

c $\frac{1}{8}\boldsymbol{m} + 3 = 2r$ ............................................ [2]

d $\boldsymbol{p} - \frac{q}{r} = s$ ............................................ [2]

e $\frac{p}{-\boldsymbol{q}} + r = -s$ ............................................ [2]

# 12 Algebraic indices

## Exercises 12.1–12.2

**1** Simplify the following using indices:

**a** $a^5 \times a^3 \times b^5 \times b^4 \times c^2$ ............................................................. [2]

**b** $p^4 \times q^7 \times p^3 \times q^2 \times r$ ............................................................. [2]

**c** $m^9 \div m^2 \div (m^2)^4 \times m^2$ ............................................................. [2]

**d** $a^5 \times e^3 \times b^5 \times e^4 \times e^2 \times e^5 \div e^{13}$ ............................................................. [2]

**2** Simplify:

**a** $ac^5 \times ac^3$ ............................................................. [2]

**b** $m^4n \div nm^2$ ............................................................. [2]

**c** $(b^3)^3 \div b^8$ ............................................................. [2]

**d** $3(2b^3)^3$ ............................................................. [2]

**e** $(c^3)^4 \times (c^6)^{-2}$ ............................................................. [2]

## Exercise 12.3

**1** Simplify the following using indices:

**a** $a^{-2} \times a^5$ ................................... [1]    **b** $(p^{-2})^3$ ............................................ [1]

**c** $(m^4)^{-2} \times m^8$ ............................................................. [2]

**2** Simplify the following using indices:

**a** $\dfrac{p^{-3} \times p^2}{p^4}$ ............................................................. [2]

**b** $\dfrac{(t^3 \times t^2)^{-2}}{t^2}$ ............................................................. [2]

**c** $\dfrac{4(r^2 \times r^{-3})^{-2}}{r^4}$ ............................................................. [3]

# 13 Equations

## Exercises 13.1–13.2

**1** Solve the following linear equations:

   **a** $4a = 12 + 3a$ ................................................................................................ [1]

   **b** $5 = 17 + 4b$ ................................................................................................ [1]

**2** Solve $3c - 9 = 5c + 13$

   .......................................................................................................................... [2]

**3** Solve the following linear equations:

   **a** $\dfrac{d}{7} = 2$ ................................................................................................ [1]

   **b** $\dfrac{e}{3} - 2 = 4$ ................................................................................................ [2]

   **c** $\dfrac{3f}{5} - 1 = 5$ ................................................................................................ [2]

   **d** $\dfrac{2g - 1}{3} = 3$ ................................................................................................ [2]

   **e** $\dfrac{4(h + 5)}{3} = 12$ ................................................................................................ [2]

**4** Solve these linear equations:

   **a** $\dfrac{7 - 2j}{5} = \dfrac{11 - 3j}{8}$ ................................................................................................ [3]

   **b** $3(2k + 4) = 2(5k - 4)$ ................................................................................................ [3]

**Photocopying prohibited**               *Cambridge IGCSE® Core Mathematics Workbook*

# Exercise 13.3

**1** The triangle has angles $x°$, $x°$ and $(x + 30)°$. Find the value of each angle.

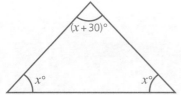

............................................................. [3]

**2** The triangle has angles $x°$, $(x + 40)°$ and $(2x - 20)°$. Find the value of each angle.

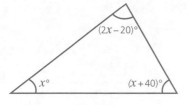

............................................................. [3]

**3** The isosceles triangle has its equal sides of length $(3x + 20)$ cm and $(4x - 5)$ cm. Calculate the value of $x$.

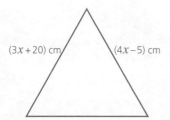

............................................................. [3]

**4** Two straight lines cross with opposite angles of $(7x + 4)°$ and $(9x - 32)°$. Calculate the size of all four angles.

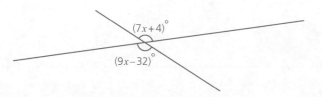

............................................................. [3]

**5** The area of a rectangle is $432 \text{ cm}^2$. Its length is three times its width. Draw a diagram and work out the size of the sides.

..................................................................................................... [3]

**6** Calculate the angles in the following:

**a**

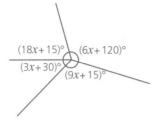

............................................................... [4]

**b**

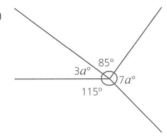

............................................................... [4]

**c**

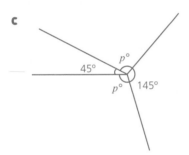

............................................................... [3]

**d**

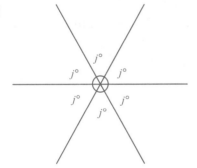

............................................................... [2]

**e**

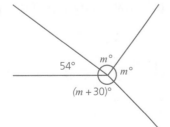

............................................................... [3]

**7** A right-angled triangle has two acute angles of $(4x - 45)°$ and $(9x - 60)°$. Calculate their size in degrees.

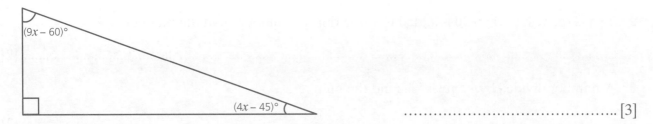

..............................................[3]

**8** A pentagon has angles $(4x + 20)°$, $(x + 40)°$, $(3x - 50)°$, $(3x - 130)°$ and $110°$. Find the value of each angle.

*The interior angles of a regular pentagon add up to 540°.*

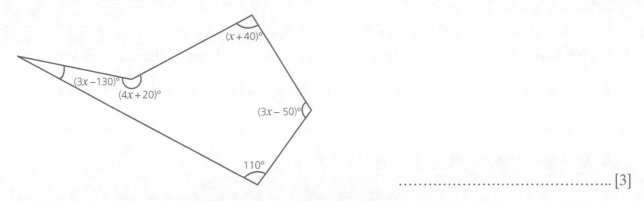

..............................................[3]

**9** An isosceles trapezium has angles as shown. Find the value of $x$.

..............................................[3]

## Exercise 13.4

**1** A number is trebled, then four is added. The total is −17. Find the number.

..............................................................................................................................[2]

**2** Two is the result when 20 is added to three times a number. Find the number.

..............................................................................................................................[2]

**3** A number divided by 17 gives −4. Find the number.

..............................................................................................................................[2]

**4** A number squared, divided by 5, less 1, is 44. Find two possible values for the number.




..............................................................................................................................[5]

**5** Zach is two years older than his sister, Leda, and three years younger than his dog, Spot.

   **a** Where Zach's age is $x$, write expressions for the ages of Leda and Spot in terms of $x$.

..............................................................................................................................[2]

   **b** Find their ages if their total age is 22 years.

..............................................................................................................................[2]

**6** A decagon has five equal exterior angles, whilst the other angles are three times bigger. Find the size of the two different angles.



..............................................................................................................................[4]

**7** A triangle has interior angles of $x°$, $2x°$ and $6x°$. Find the size of its exterior angles.

..............................................................[4]

**8** A number squared has the number squared then doubled added to it. The total is 300. Find two possible values for the number.




..............................................................................................................................[4]

# Exercise 13.5

Solve these simultaneous equations:

**a**    $a + b = 12$
     $a - b = 2$

........................................................ [2]

**b**    $3c + d = 19$
     $3c + 4d = 49$

........................................................ [3]

**c**    $7e + 4f = 56$
     $e + 4f = 32$

........................................................ [3]

**d**    $g + h = -12$
     $g - h = 2$

........................................................ [2]

**e**    $-5p - 3q = -24$
     $-5p + 3q = -6$

........................................................ [3]

**f**    $2r - 3s = 0$
     $2r + 4s = -14$

........................................................ [3]

**g**    $w + x = 0$
     $w - x = 10$

........................................................ [2]

**h**    $x + y = 2$
     $x - y = 1$

........................................................ [2]

# Exercise 13.6

Solve these simultaneous equations:

**a**    $2a + 3b = 12$
     $a + b = 5$

........................................................ [3]

**b**    $3c - 3d = 12$
     $2c + d = 11$

........................................................ [3]

**c**    $e - f = 0$
     $4e + 2f = -6$

........................................................ [3]

**d**    $12g + 6y = 15$
     $g + 2y = 2$

........................................................ [3]

**e**    $4h + j = 14$
     $12h - 6j = 6$

........................................................ [4]

**f**    $100k - 10l = -20$
     $-15k + 3l = 9$

........................................................ [2]

**g** $-3 = m + n$
$m - n = 11$

**h** $3 - p = q$
$3 - q = 2$

.................................................... [3]          .................................................... [3]

**i** $3r - 2s = 26$
$4s + 2 = r$

**j** $\frac{1}{2}t + 2w = 1$
$4w - t = 0$

.................................................... [4]          .................................................... [4]

## Exercise 13.7

**1** The sum of two numbers is 37 and their difference is 11. Find the numbers.

.................................................................................[3]

**2** The sum of two numbers is –2 and their difference is 12. Find the numbers.

.................................................................................[3]

**3** If a girl multiplies her age in years by four and adds three times her brother's age, she gets 64. If the boy adds his age in years to double his sister's age, he gets 28. How old are they?

.................................................................................[4]

**4** A rectangle has opposite sides of $3a + b$ and 25 and $2a + 3b$ and 26. Find the values of $a$ and $b$.

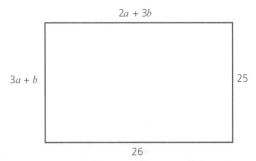

[4]

**5** A square has sides $2x$, $40 - 3x$, $25 + 3y$ and $10 - 2y$. Calculate:

**a** the values of $x$ and $y$

..................................................................................................................................[2]

**b** the area of the square

..................................................................................................................................[3]

**c** the perimeter of the square.

..................................................................................................................................[2]

**6** A grandmother is four times as old as her granddaughter. She is also 48 years older than her. How old are they both?

..................................................................................................................................[3]

# 14 Sequences

## Exercises 14.1–14.2

**1** Give the next two terms in each sequence.

   **a** 17, 20, 23, 26, ____, ____   [1]   **b** 2, 5, 10, 17, ____, ____  [1]   **c** 5, 13, 21, 29, ____, ____  [1]

**2 a** Draw the next two patterns in the sequence below.

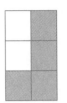 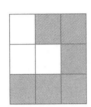 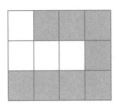

[2]

   **b** Complete the table below linking the number of white squares to the number of shaded squares.

| Number of white squares | 2 | 3 | 4 | 5 | 6 |
|---|---|---|---|---|---|
| Number of shaded squares | | | | | |

[2]

   **c** Write the rule for the $n$th term for the sequence of shaded squares.

     .............................................................................................................................................[2]

   **d** Use your rule to predict the number of shaded squares in a pattern with 50 white squares.

     .............................................................................................................................................[2]

**3** For each sequence, calculate the next two terms and explain the pattern in words.

   **a** 9, 16, 25, 36

     .............................................................................................................................................[4]

   **b** 2, 6, 12, 20, 30, 42

     .............................................................................................................................................[4]

**4** For each sequence, give an expression for the $n$th term.

   **a** 7, 11, 15, 19 .............................................................................................................[2]

   **b** 7, 9, 11, 13 .............................................................................................................[2]

   **c** 3, 6, 11, 18 .............................................................................................................[2]

## Exercises 14.3–14.4

**1** For each sequence: **i** give the next two terms; **ii** find the formula for the $n$th term. Use a table if necessary.

    **a**   0, 7, 26, 63, 124

       **i** ...................................................................................................................................... [2]

      **ii** ...................................................................................................................................... [2]

    **b**   3, 10, 29, 66, 127

       **i** ...................................................................................................................................... [3]

      **ii** ...................................................................................................................................... [3]

**2** Complete the table to show the first eight square and cube numbers.

| $n$ | 1 | 2 | 3 | 4 | 5 | 6 | 7 | 8 | |
|-----|---|---|---|---|---|---|---|---|---|
| $n^2$ | | | 9 | | | | | | [1] |
| $n^3$ | | | 27 | | | | | | [1] |

**3** The first seven terms of the Fibonacci sequence are 1, 1, 2, 3, 5, 8, 13.

    **a**   What are the next two numbers? ......................................................................... [1]

    **b**   Explain, in words, the rule for this sequence.

        ...................................................................................................................................... [1]

**4** For each sequence, consider its relation to the sequences of square, cube or triangular numbers, then: **i** write down the next two terms; **ii** write down the expression for the $n$th term.

    **a**   –1, 2, 7, 14, 23

       **i** ...................................................................................................................................... [2]

      **ii** ...................................................................................................................................... [2]

    **b**   0, 2, 5, 9, 14

       **i** ...................................................................................................................................... [2]

      **ii** ...................................................................................................................................... [2]

    **c**   $\frac{1}{4}, 2, 6\frac{3}{4}, 16, 31\frac{1}{4}$

       **i** ...................................................................................................................................... [2]

      **ii** ...................................................................................................................................... [2]

# 15 Graphs in practical situations

## Exercise 15.1

**1** Water is charged at $0.20 per unit.

   **a** Draw a conversion graph on the axes below up to 50 units.

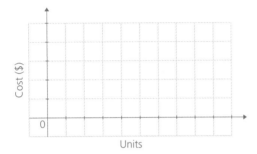

[3]

   **b** From your graph, estimate the cost of using 23 units of water. Show your method clearly.

   .................................................................................................................................[2]

   **c** From your graph, estimate the number of units used if the cost was $7.50. Show your method clearly.

   .................................................................................................................................[2]

**2** A Science exam is marked out of 180.

   **a** Draw a conversion graph to change the marks to percentages.

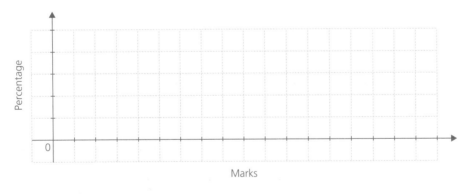

[3]

   **b** Using the graph and showing your method clearly, estimate the percentage score if a student achieved a mark of 130.

   .................................................................................................................................[2]

   **c** Using the graph and showing your method clearly, estimate the actual mark if a student got 35%.

   .................................................................................................................................[2]

## Exercise 15.2

**1** Find the average speed of an object moving:

   **a** 60 m in 12 s ................................................................................................................ [1]

   **b** 140 km in 1 h 20 min. ................................................................................................ [2]

**2** How far will an object travel during:

   **a** 25 s at 32 m/s ............................................................................................................. [1]

   **b** 2 h 18 min at 15 m/s? ................................................................................................. [2]

**3** How long will an object take to travel:

   **a** 2.5 km at 20 km/h ...................................................................................................... [1]

   **b** 4.8 km at 48 m/s? ....................................................................................................... [2]

## Exercises 15.3–15.4

**1** Two people, A and B, set off from points 300 m apart and travel towards each other along a straight road. Their movement is shown on the graph below:

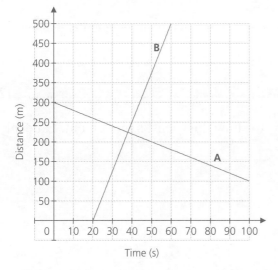

   **a** Calculate the speed of person A.

   .................................................................................................................................... [2]

   **b** Calculate the speed of person B when she is moving.

   .................................................................................................................................... [2]

**c** Use the graph to estimate how far apart they are 50 seconds after person A has set off.

..............................................................................................................................................[2]

**d** Explain the motion of person B in the first 20 seconds.

..............................................................................................................................................[1]

**e** Calculate the average speed of person B during the first 60 seconds.

..............................................................................................................................................[2]

**2** A cyclist sets off at 09 00 one morning and does the following:

- Stage 1: Cycles for 30 minutes at a speed of 20 km/h.
- Stage 2: Rests for 15 minutes.
- Stage 3: Cycles again at a speed of 30 km/h for 30 minutes.
- Stage 4: Rests for another 15 minutes.
- Stage 5: Realises his front wheel has a puncture so walks with the bicycle for 30 minutes at a speed of 5 km/h to his destination.

  **a** At what time does the cyclist reach his destination?

  ..............................................................................................................................................[2]

  **b** How far does he travel during stage 1?

  ..............................................................................................................................................[2]

  **c** Draw a distance–time graph on the axes below to show the cyclist's movement. Label all five stages clearly on the graph.

  Distance (km) / Time (minutes)

  [5]

  **d** Calculate the cyclist's average speed for the whole journey. Answer in km/h.

  ..............................................................................................................................................[2]

# 16 Graphs of functions

## Exercise 16.1
Plot the following straight lines on the axes given:

**a** $y = \frac{1}{2}x - 1$ [2]

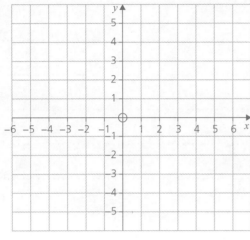

| x | y |
|---|---|
|   |   |
|   |   |
|   |   |

**b** $y + 2x = 4$ [2]

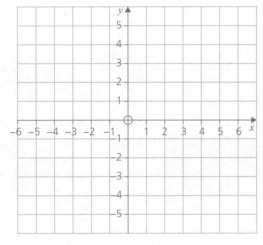

| x | y |
|---|---|
|   |   |
|   |   |
|   |   |

**c** $x + 2y + 4 = 0$ [3]

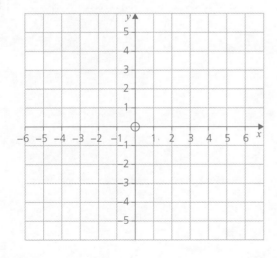

| x | y |
|---|---|
|   |   |
|   |   |
|   |   |

## Exercise 16.2

Solve the simultaneous equations: **i** by graphical means; **ii** by algebraic means.

**a** $y - 2x = -3$
$4y + 2x = 8$

**i**
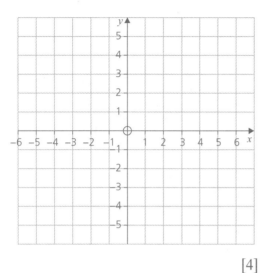

[4]

**ii** ......................................................
......................................................
......................................................
......................................................
......................................................
......................................................
......................................................[4]

**b** $y + x - 3 = 0$
$y = -3x + 1$

**i**
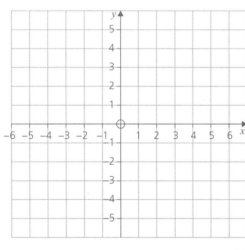

[4]

**ii** ......................................................
......................................................
......................................................
......................................................
......................................................
......................................................
......................................................[4]

# Exercise 16.3

For each of the following quadratic functions, complete the table of values and draw the graph on the grid provided:

**a** $y = x^2 + 6x + 8$

| $x$ | –5 | –4 | –3 | –2 | –1 |
|-----|----|----|----|----|----|
| $y$ |    |    |    |    |    |

[2]

**b** $y = -x^2 + 3x + 4$

| $x$ | –2 | –1 | 0 | 1 | 2 | 3 | 4 | 5 |
|-----|----|----|---|---|---|---|---|---|
| $y$ |    |    |   |   |   |   |   |   |

[2]

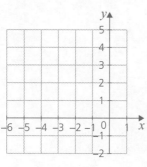

[2]

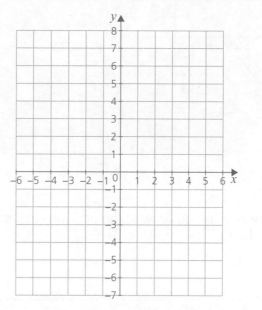

[2]

# Exercise 16.4

Solve each of the following quadratic functions by plotting a graph of the function:

**a** $x^2 - 4x - 5 = 0$

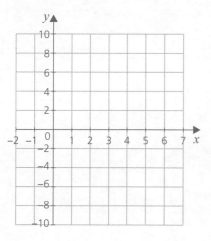

[3]

$x =$ ............................................. [2]

**b** $-x^2 + 8x - 12 = 0$

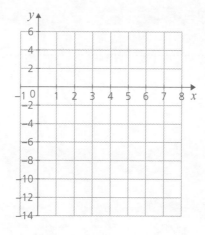

[3]

$x =$ ................................................. [2]

c   $-x^2 - 3x + 10 = 0$

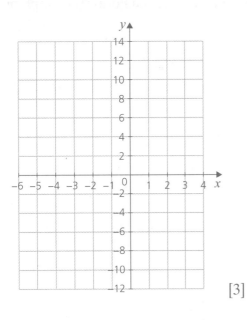

[3]                                              $x = $ .............................................. [2]

## Exercise 16.5

Using the graphs you drew in the previous exercise, solve these quadratic equations. Show your method clearly.

a   $x^2 - 4x - 13 = 0$

.......................................................................................................... [2]

b   $-x^2 + 8x = 0$

.......................................................................................................... [2]

c   $-x^2 - 3x + 14 = 0$

.......................................................................................................... [2]

## Exercise 16.6

Complete the table of values and draw on the grid provided the graph
of the reciprocal function $y = \dfrac{3}{2x}$.

| $x$ | $-4$ | $-3$ | $-2$ | $-1$ | 0 | 1 | 2 | 3 | 4 |
|-----|------|------|------|------|---|---|---|---|---|
| $y$ |      |      |      |      |   |   |   |   |   |

[2]

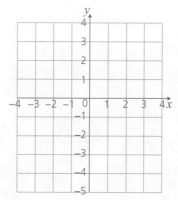

[2]

## Exercise 16.7

Sketch the following linear functions, showing clearly where the lines intersect both axes:

**a** $x + y = 5$ **b** $2x - y - 5 = 0$

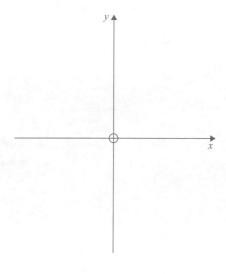

[3]

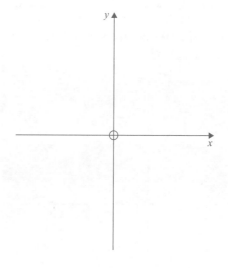

[3]

## Exercise 16.8

**1** The quadratic equation $y = x^2 - 3x - 4$ has a turning point at $\left(\frac{5}{2}, -\frac{21}{4}\right)$. Sketch the quadratic on the axes.

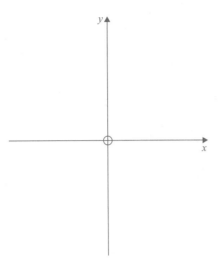

[2]

**2 a** Expand $y = -(x - 2)(x - 6)$

.................................................................................................................................[2]

**b** Use your expansion to sketch the graph of $y = -(x - 2)(x - 6)$. Mark the intersections with both axes clearly.

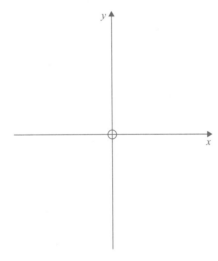

[3]

# 17 Coordinates and straight line graphs

## Exercises 17.1–17.3

**1 a** On the axes below, plot and join the points in alphabetical order.

$A(1, 2)$

$B(-2, 3)$

$C(-1, 0)$

$D(4, -3)$

**b** Name the quadrilateral produced.

..............................................[1]

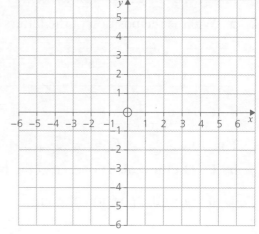

[2]

**2 a** On the axes (right), draw a circle with the centre at $(-3, 2)$ and a radius of 5 units. Draw a second circle with the centre at $(4, 3)$ and also with a radius of 5 units.

**b** Give the coordinates of the two points of intersection of the circles.

........................ and

....................... [2]

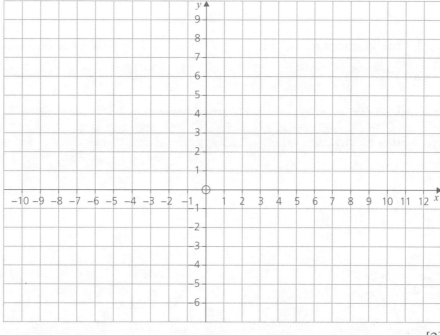

[2]

# Exercises 17.4–17.5

1 What is the position of letters A, B, C and D on the scale below?

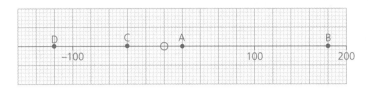

A = ................    B = ................    C = ................    D = ................      [4]

2 **a** What is the position of the letters P, Q, R and S on the scale below?

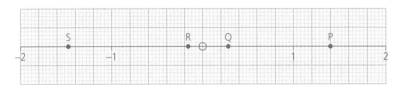

P = ................    Q = ................    R = ................    S = ................      [4]

   **b**   **i**   On the scale above, label the point T that is midway between P and Q.     [1]

         **ii**   Give the position of point T. ...................................................................[1]

# Exercises 17.6–17.8

1 In each of the following, identify the coordinates of some of the points on the line and use these to find:

   **i**   the gradient of the line          **ii**   the equation of the straight line.

   **a**

     **i**   ................................................... [1]

     **ii**   ................................................... [1]

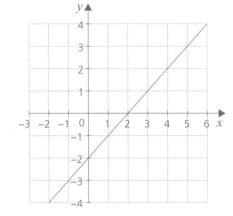

   **b**

     **i**   ................................................... [1]

     **ii**   ................................................... [1]

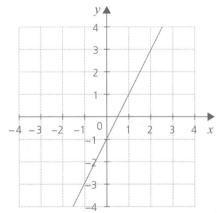

**c**

  **i** .................................................... [1]

  **ii** .................................................... [1]

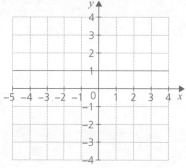

**d**

  **i** .................................................... [1]

  **ii** .................................................... [1]

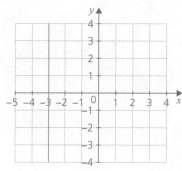

**e**

  **i** .................................................... [1]

  **ii** .................................................... [1]

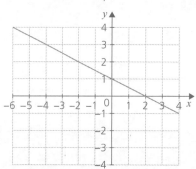

**2** In each of the following, identify the coordinates of some of the points on the line and use these to find the equation of the straight line:

**a**

  .................................................

  .................................................

  ................................................. [3]

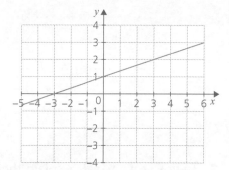

**b**

........................................................

........................................................

........................................................ [3]

**c**

........................................................

........................................................

........................................................ [3]

**d**

........................................................

........................................................

........................................................ [3]

**e**

........................................................

........................................................

........................................................ [4]

3  In your own words, explain the significance of '*m*' and '*c*' in the equation of a straight line.

*The general equation of a straight line takes the form* $y = mx + c$.

........................................................................................................................

........................................................................................................................ [3]

## Exercise 17.9

For the following linear equations, calculate both the gradient and $y$-intercept:

**a** $y = 4x - 2$

......................................................

.................................................... [2]

**b** $y = -(2x + 6)$

......................................................

.................................................... [4]

**c** $y + \frac{1}{2}x = 3$

......................................................

.................................................... [3]

**d** $y - (4 - 3x) = 0$

......................................................

.................................................... [4]

**e** $\frac{1}{2}y + x - 2 = 0$

......................................................

.................................................... [4]

**f** $-5y - 1 - 10x = 0$

......................................................

.................................................... [4]

**g** $-\frac{4}{3}y + 2x = 4$

......................................................

.................................................... [4]

**h** $\frac{3x - 2y}{5} = -3$

......................................................

.................................................... [4]

## Exercises 17.10–17.11

**1** Write down the equation of any two lines that are parallel to the line $y = 4x + 7$.

**i** ................................................................................ [1]

**ii** ................................................................................ [1]

**2** Find the equation of the straight line parallel to $y = -2x + 6$ that passes through the point $(2, 5)$.

......................................................

.................................................... [2]

# 18 Geometrical vocabulary

## Exercises 18.1–18.4

**1** Define:

    **a** an obtuse angle

    ..................................................................................................................................[1]

    **b** a reflex angle.

    ..................................................................................................................................[1]

**2** What is:

    **a** the complementary angle of 25°

    ..................................................................................................................................[1]

    **b** the supplementary angle of 125°?

    ..................................................................................................................................[1]

**3** **a** Draw an obtuse-angled triangle PQR.

    [2]

    **b** Name each of the angles in terms of three vertices.

    …….....................…… [1]    …….....................…… [1]    …….....................…… [1]

**4** Draw and label these lines.

    **a** A pair of parallel lines        **b** A pair of perpendicular lines

    …….................................................…… [1]    …….................................................…… [1]

**5** Sketch a regular pentagon.

    [2]

     *Cambridge IGCSE® Core Mathematics Workbook*

## Exercise 18.5

**1** Three nets A, B and C are shown. Tick which (if any) can be folded to make a cube.

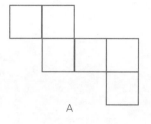
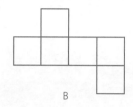
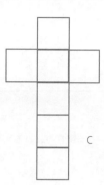

[2]

**2** On each of the nets below, a face has been marked with an X. If the cubes were assembled, mark, with a Y, the face that would be opposite X.

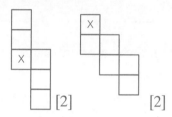

[2]          [2]

## Exercise 18.6

**1** Examine these triangles:

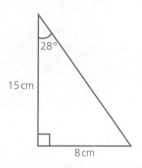
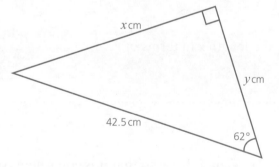

  **a** Explain why the two triangles are similar.

  ...................................................................................................................................[2]

  **b** Calculate the scale factor that enlarges the smaller triangle to the larger triangle.

  ...................................................................................................................................[3]

  **c** Calculate the value of *x*.

  ...................................................................................................................................[2]

  **d** Calculate the value of *y*.

  ...................................................................................................................................[2]

**2**

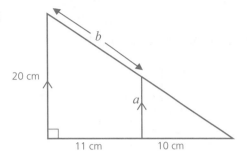

**a** Calculate the length $a$ to 4 s.f.

.................................................................................................................[2]

**b** Calculate the length $b$ to 4 s.f.

.................................................................................................................[3]

**3** The diagram shows two arcs with the same centre and an angle $\theta$.

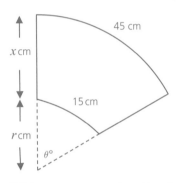

Write an expression for the length $x$ in terms of $r$.

.................................................................................................................[2]

## Exercise 18.7

In the grid below, complete the second shape so that it is congruent to shape A.

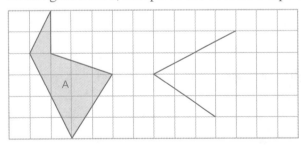

[2]

# Geometrical constructions and scale drawings

## Exercises 19.1–19.3

**1** In triangle PQR, measure each angle to the nearest degree and each side to the nearest mm.

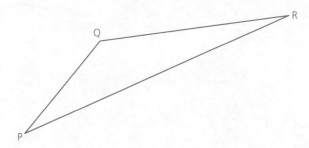

Angle *PQR* ...........................................

Angle *QRP* ...........................................

Angle *RPQ* ...........................................

PQ ...........................................

QR ...........................................

RP .......................................... [2]

**2** Using only a ruler and a pair of compasses, construct the following triangle XYZ.

XY = 5 cm, XZ = 3 cm and YZ = 7 cm.

[3]

## Exercise 19.4

**1** The scale of a map is 1:20 000.

**a** Two villages are 12 cm apart on the map. How far apart are they in real life? Answer in kilometres.

.................................................................................................................. [2]

**b** The distance from a village to the edge of a lake is 8 km in real life. How far apart are they on the map? Answer in centimetres.

.................................................................................................................. [2]

**2 a** A model car is a $\frac{1}{25}$ scale model. Express this as a ratio.

.................................................................................................................. [1]

**b** If the length of the real car is 4.9 m, what is the length of the model car?

.................................................................................................................. [1]

# 20 Symmetry

## Exercises 20.1–20.2

1 Sketch each of the shapes below and show their lines of symmetry.

    **a** A regular dodecagon          **b** A rhombus

                                                   [3]                              [2]

2 Indicate the order of rotational symmetry for each of the shapes above.

    **a**                                                   **b**

       ……………………………………………. [1]      ……………………………………………… [1]

# 21 Angle properties

## Exercise 21.1

**1** In each of the diagrams below, the angles lie on a straight line. Calculate the value of *x*.

**a**

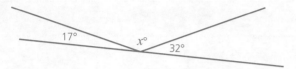

.................................................... [1]

**b**

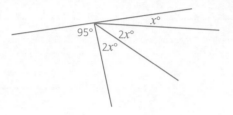

....................................................[3]

**2** In the diagram below, the angles lie about a point. Calculate the value of *p*.

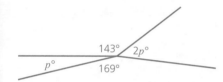

....................................................[2]

## Exercises 21.2–21.7

**1** Calculate the size of each of the labelled angles.

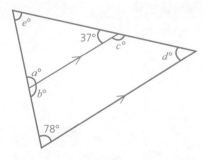

*a* = ....................................................[1]

*b* = ....................................................[1]

*c* = ....................................................[1]

*d* = ....................................................[1]

*e* = ....................................................[1]

**2** Calculate the size of the labelled angles in the kite.

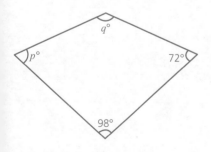

*p* = ....................................................[1]

*q* = ....................................................[2]

## Exercise 21.8

Complete the table below. Enter 'Yes' or 'No' in each cell.

| | Rhombus | Parallelogram | Kite |
|---|---|---|---|
| Opposite sides equal in length | | | |
| All sides equal in length | | | |
| All angles right angles | | | |
| Both pairs of opposite sides parallel | | | |
| Diagonals equal in length | | | |
| Diagonals intersect at right angles | | | |
| All angles equal | | | |

[3]

## Exercises 21.9–21.10

1  The size of each interior angle of a regular polygon is 165°. Calculate:

  **a**  the size of each exterior angle ............................................................... [1]

  **b**  the number of sides of the regular polygon

    ................................................................................................. [2]

2  Find the value of each interior angle of a regular polygon with:

  **a**  30 sides ............................................................................... [2]

  **b**  20 sides. .............................................................................. [2]

**3** Calculate the number of sides of a regular polygon if each interior angle is $4x°$ and each exterior angle is $x°$.

.................................................................................................................................... [3]

**4** The pentagon below has angles as shown:

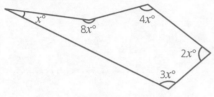

**a** State the sum of the interior angles of a pentagon. ....................................................... [1]

**b** Calculate the value of $x$.

................................................................................................................................ [2]

**c** Calculate the size of each of the angles of the pentagon.

................................................................................................................................ [2]

**5** The diagram shows an octagon.

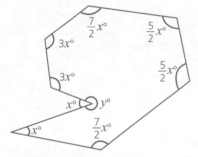

**a** Write the angle $y$ in terms of $x$. ................................................................................. [1]

**b** Write an equation for the sum of the interior angles of the octagon in terms of $x$.

................................................................................................................................ [2]

**c** Calculate the value of $x$.

................................................................................................................................ [2]

**d** Calculate the size of the angle labelled $y$. ................................................................ [1]

## Exercise 21.11

In the diagram, O marks the centre of the circle. Calculate the value of $x$.

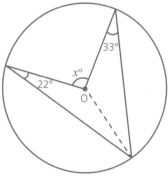

.................................................................................................................... [2]

## Exercise 21.12

In each diagram, O marks the centre of the circle. Calculate the value of the labelled angles in each case.

**a**

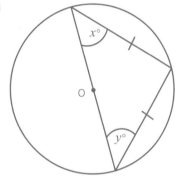

.................................................................................................................... [2]

**b**

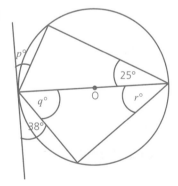

.................................................................................................................... [3]

# 22 Measures

## Exercises 22.1–22.4

1 Convert these lengths to the units indicated:

   **a** 0.072 m to mm ................................................................................... [1]

   **b** 20 400 m to km ................................................................................... [1]

2 Convert these masses to the units indicated:

   **a** 420 g to kg ....................................................................................... [1]

   **b** 1.04 tonnes to kg ............................................................................... [1]

3 Convert these liquid measures to the units indicated:

   **a** 12 ml to litres ................................................................................... [1]

   **b** 0.24 litres to ml ................................................................................ [1]

4 Calculate the sum of the following four volumes and convert your answer to litres:

440 ml                  870 ml                  1650 ml                 540 ml

.................................................................................................. [2]

5 Convert these measures to the units indicated:

   **a** 150 mm$^2$ to cm$^2$ ............................................................................ [1]

   **b** 50 000 m$^2$ to km$^2$ ......................................................................... [1]

   **c** 3 m$^3$ to cm$^3$ ................................................................................. [1]

   **d** 400 cm$^3$ to litres ............................................................................ [1]

# 23 Perimeter, area and volume

## Exercises 23.1–23.6

**1** Find the area and perimeter of the following shapes:

**a** A rectangle 4.5 cm by 3.5 cm

Area ............................. [1]        Perimeter ........................... [1]

**b** A right-angled triangle of base 1.5 cm, height 2 cm and hypotenuse 2.5 cm.

Area ............................. [1]        Perimeter ........................... [1]

**2** Calculate the shaded area of the compound shape.

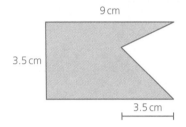

Area ............................. [3]

**3** The rectangle and trapezium have the same area. Calculate the value of *x*.

 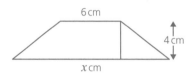

...................................................................................................... [4]

## Exercises 23.7–23.8

**1** Calculate the circumference and area of the circle.

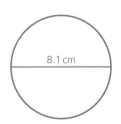

Circumference ........................... [1]   Area ........................... [1]

**2** A circle has an area of $12.25\pi\,\text{cm}^2$. Calculate:

**a** its diameter ................................................................................[2]

**b** its circumference ..........................................................................[2]

**3** A semi-circular shape is removed from a trapezium shape as shown:

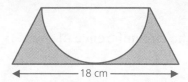

If the semicircle has a radius of 7 cm, calculate the shaded area remaining.

.................................................................................................[3]

**4** A trapezium and parallelogram are joined as shown:

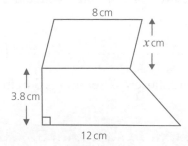

If the total area is $53.2\,\text{cm}^2$, calculate the value of $x$.

.................................................................................................[3]

**5** Five thin semi-circular chocolate pieces are placed in a rectangular box as shown:

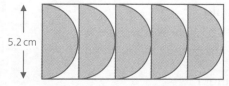

Calculate:

**a** the length of the box

.................................................................................................[2]

**b** the area occupied by one piece of chocolate

.................................................................................................[2]

**c** the area of the box not covered by chocolate pieces.

.................................................................................................[2]

**6** A circular hole is cut out of a circular shape as shown:

The area remaining is the same as the area of the hole removed. The circumference of the original piece is $15\pi$ cm. Calculate the radius of the circular hole.

.................................................................................................................................................. [4]

## Exercises 23.9–23.12

**1** A cuboid has a length of 7 cm, a width of 2.5 cm and a total surface area of 114.8 cm². Calculate its height.

.................................................................................................................................................. [2]

**2** A cylinder has a total surface area of 100 cm². If the radius of its circular cross-section is 3.6 cm, calculate its height.

.................................................................................................................................................. [2]

**3** A cylinder and a cuboid have dimensions as shown:

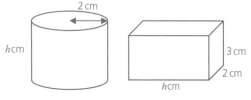

    **a** Write an expression for the total surface area of the cuboid.

    .............................................................................................................................................. [2]

    **b** Write an expression for the total surface area of the cylinder.

    .............................................................................................................................................. [2]

    **c** If the total surface area of the cylinder is twice that of the cuboid, find the value of $h$.

    .............................................................................................................................................. [3]

**4** A metal hand weight is made from two cubes and a cylinder joined as shown:

8 cm    8 cm    8 cm

Calculate the volume of the shape.

............................................................................................................................................[3]

**5** A cylinder and a cylindrical pipe have the same volume and diameter.

9 cm

12 cm          30 cm          $x$ cm

**a** Calculate the volume of the solid cylinder. Give your answer in terms of $\pi$.

............................................................................................................................................[2]

**b** Write an expression for the volume of the cylindrical pipe.

............................................................................................................................................[3]

**c** Calculate the value of $x$.

............................................................................................................................................[3]

## Exercises 23.13–23.14

**1** A sector has a radius of 6 cm and an arc length of $\frac{2}{3}\pi$ cm. Calculate the angle of the sector $\theta$.

............................................................................................................................................[2]

**2** A sector has an angle of 120° and an arc length of 14 cm. Calculate the length of the sector's radius, giving your answer in terms of $\pi$.

............................................................................................................................................[2]

## Exercises 23.15–23.16

**1** Two sectors, A and B, are shown below:

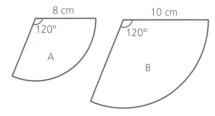

**a** Calculate the area of sector A. Give your answer in terms of π.

......................................................................................................................................................[1]

**b** What is the ratio of the areas of sectors A:B? Give your answer in the form 1:$n$.

......................................................................................................................................................[2]

**2** A prism with a cross-section in the shape of a sector is shown below:

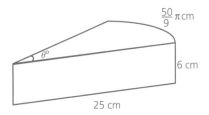

Calculate:

**a** the angle $\theta$ ..................................................................................................................................[1]

**b** in terms of π, the area of the cross-section

......................................................................................................................................................[2]

**c** the total surface area of the prism, to the nearest whole number

......................................................................................................................................................[3]

**d** in terms of π, the volume of the prism.

......................................................................................................................................................[1]

## Exercises 23.17–23.18

**1** A sphere has a volume of $0.5\,\text{m}^3$. Calculate the sphere's radius, giving your answer in cm to 1 d.p.

......................................................................................................................................................[2]

**2** The diagram below shows a sphere of radius 3 cm and an open-topped container in the shape of a cube of side length 10 cm. The container is filled with water to a depth of 6 cm.

 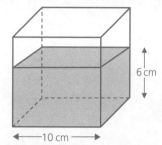

**a** Calculate the volume of the sphere, giving your answer in terms of π.

.....................................................................................................................................................[2]

**b** The sphere is submerged in the water. Determine whether the water spills over the rim of the container. You must show your working to justify your answer.

.....................................................................................................................................................[2]

**c** The sphere is removed. Another sphere of radius $r$ cm is submerged in the container. Show that the increase in height ($h$ cm) of the level of water in the container is given by $h = \dfrac{\pi r^3}{75}$

.....................................................................................................................................................[3]

# Exercise 23.19

**1** A hemisphere has a radius of 5 cm.

**a** Calculate, in terms of π, the area of its flat base.

.....................................................................................................................................................[1]

**b** Calculate, in terms of π, its total surface area.

.....................................................................................................................................................[3]

**2** A solid shape is made from two hemispheres joined together.

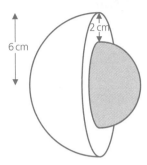

The base of each hemisphere shares the same centre.

**a** Calculate the surface area of the smaller hemisphere.

.......................................................................................................................................[2]

**b** Calculate the total surface area of the shape.

.......................................................................................................................................[4]

## Exercises 23.20–23.21

**1** A rectangular-based pyramid is shown:

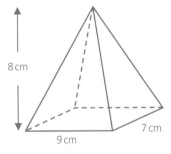

**a** Calculate the volume of the pyramid.

.......................................................................................................................................[2]

**b** Calculate the total surface area of the pyramid, using Pythagoras' theorem.

.......................................................................................................................................[4]

**2** Two square-based pyramids are joined at their bases. The bases have an edge length of 6 cm.

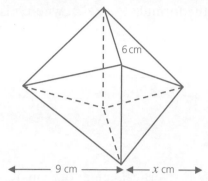

6 cm

◄── 9 cm ──►◄── *x* cm ──►

**a** Calculate the volume of the pyramid on the left.

............................................................................................................[2]

**b** If the volume of the pyramid on the left is twice that of the pyramid on the right, calculate the value of *x*.

............................................................................................................[2]

**c** By using Pythagoras as part of the calculation, calculate the total surface area of the shape.

............................................................................................................[4]

## Exercises 23.22–23.24

**1** A cone has a base diameter of 8 cm and a sloping face length of 5 cm.

**a** Calculate its perpendicular height.

............................................................................................................[2]

**b** Calculate the volume of the cone.

............................................................................................................[2]

**c** Calculate the total surface area of the cone.

............................................................................................................[4]

2 The curved surface area ($A$) of a cone is given by the formula $A = rl$, where $r$ is the base radius and $l$ is the slant length. The volume ($V$) of a cone is given by the formula $V = \pi r^2 \frac{h}{3}$, where $r$ is the base radius and $h$ is the vertical height.

A *solid* cone has a slant length of 10 cm, a base radius of 6 cm and a vertical height of 8 cm. It is bisected and one half is kept, as shown.

a Calculate the area of the triangular face of the bisected shape.

..................................................................................................................................[2]

b Calculate the volume of the bisected shape. Give your answer correct to 3 s.f.

..................................................................................................................................[3]

c Calculate the total surface area of the bisected shape. Give your answer correct to 3 s.f.

..................................................................................................................................[4]

# 24 Bearings

## Exercises 24.1–24.2

A boat sets off from a point A on a bearing of 130° for 4 km to a point B. At B it changes direction and sails on a bearing of 240° to a point C, 7 km away. At point C it changes direction again and heads back to point A.

**a** Using a scale of 1 cm : 1 km, draw a scale diagram of the boat's journey.

[4]

**b** From your diagram work out:

**i** the distance AC ................................................................................................ [1]

**ii** the bearing of A from C.

.................................................................................................................................. [2]

**c** Without measuring, deduce the bearing of A from B. Explain clearly how you calculate your answer.

.................................................................................................................................. [2]

# 25 Right-angled triangles

## Exercises 25.1–25.3

Calculate the value of $x$ in each triangle. Give your answers to 1 d.p.

**a**
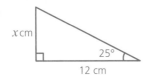

$x$ cm, 25°, 12 cm

.................................................... [2]

**b**
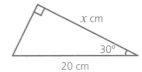

$x$ cm, 30°, 20 cm

.................................................... [2]

**c**
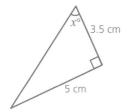

$x°$, 3.5 cm, 5 cm

.................................................... [2]

**d**
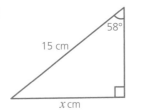

58°, 15 cm, $x$ cm

.................................................... [2]

**e**
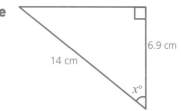

6.9 cm, 14 cm, $x°$

.................................................... [2]

**f**
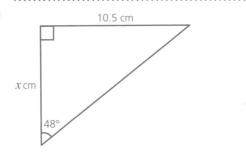

10.5 cm, $x$ cm, 48°

.................................................... [2]

**g**

$x°$, 24.1 cm, 15.6 cm

.................................................... [2]

**h**
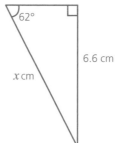

62°, 6.6 cm, $x$ cm

.................................................... [2]

          *Cambridge IGCSE® Core Mathematics Workbook*

# Exercises 25.4–25.5

**1** In each diagram, calculate the length of the marked side. Answer to 1 d.p.

**a**

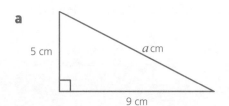

................................................... [2]

**b**

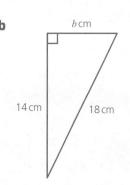

................................................... [2]

**c**

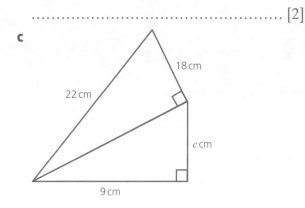

................................................... [3]

**d**

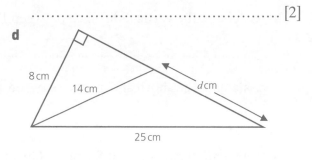

................................................... [3]

**2** Three towns, A, B and C, are positioned relative to each other as follows:

Town B is 68 km from A on a bearing of 225°.

Town C is on a bearing of 135° from A.

Town C is on a bearing of 090° from B.

**a** With the aid of a sketch if necessary, deduce the distance from A to C.

.................................................................................................... [2]

**b** Calculate the distance from B to C.

.................................................................................................... [2]

**3** A boat starts at a point P and heads due north for 20 km to a point Q. At Q it heads east for 15 km to a point R. At R it heads on a bearing of 045° for 10 km to a point S.

 **a** With the aid of a sketch if necessary, calculate the horizontal distance between R and S.

.............................................................................................................................................[2]

 **b** Calculate the vertical distance between P and S.

.............................................................................................................................................[2]

 **c** Calculate the shortest distance between P and S.

.............................................................................................................................................[2]

 **d** Calculate the bearing of S from P. Give the answer to the nearest degree.

.............................................................................................................................................[2]

**4** Two trees, A and B, are standing on flat ground 12 m apart as shown. The tops of the two trees are 16 m apart. Angle *a* is 50°.

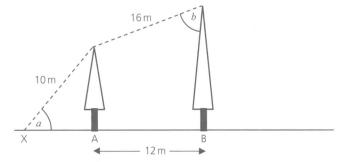

 **a** Calculate the distance AX.

.............................................................................................................................................[2]

 **b** Calculate the height of tree B.

.............................................................................................................................................[2]

 **c** Calculate angle *b*.

.............................................................................................................................................[2]

# 26 Vectors

## Exercise 26.1

Describe each of the following translations using a column vector:

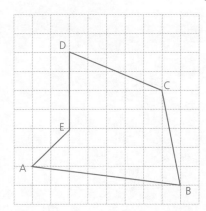

a $\overrightarrow{AB}$ ...................................................................[1]

b $\overrightarrow{BC}$ ...................................................................[1]

c $\overrightarrow{CD}$ ...................................................................[1]

d $\overrightarrow{DE}$ ...................................................................[1]

e $\overrightarrow{EA}$ ...................................................................[1]

## Exercises 26.2–26.3

In questions 1 and 2, consider the following vectors:

$$\mathbf{a} = \begin{pmatrix} 2 \\ 0 \end{pmatrix} \qquad \mathbf{b} = \begin{pmatrix} -3 \\ 1 \end{pmatrix} \qquad \mathbf{c} = \begin{pmatrix} 3 \\ -2 \end{pmatrix}$$

**1** Express the following as a single column vector:

a $3\mathbf{a}$ .................................................... [1]     b $2\mathbf{c} - \mathbf{b}$ ......................................... [2]

c $\frac{1}{2}(\mathbf{a} - \mathbf{b})$ ...................................... [2]     d $-2\mathbf{b}$ .............................................[2]

**2** Draw vector diagrams to represent the following:

a $2\mathbf{a} + \mathbf{b}$

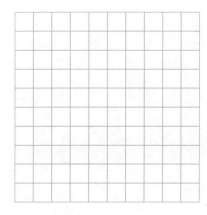

[3]

b $-\mathbf{c} + \mathbf{b}$

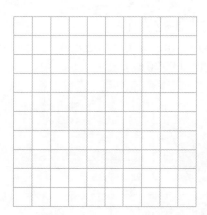

[3]

# 27 Transformations

## Exercises 27.1–27.2

**1** Draw the position of the mirror lines on the following diagrams:

**a**

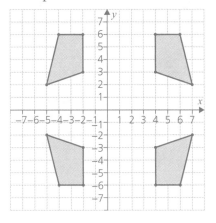

[2]

**b**

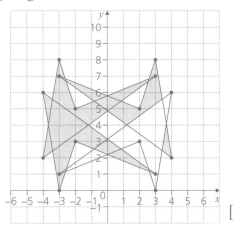

[2]

**2** Reflect the following object in the mirror line shown.

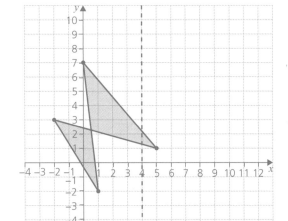

[2]

## Exercises 27.3–27.4

**1** In the following, the object and centre of rotation have been given. Draw the object's image under the stated rotation.

**a**

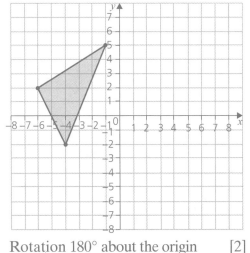

Rotation 180° about the origin        [2]

**b**

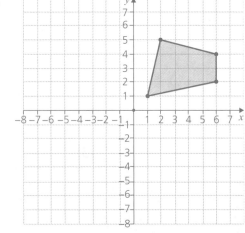

Rotation 90° anticlockwise about the origin [2]

**2** In the following, the object (unshaded) and image (shaded) have been drawn. In each diagram, mark the centre of rotation and calculate the angle and direction of rotation.

**a**

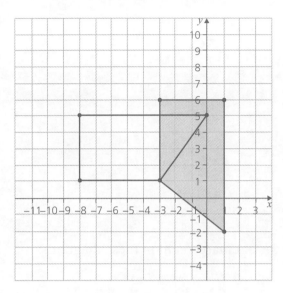

**b**

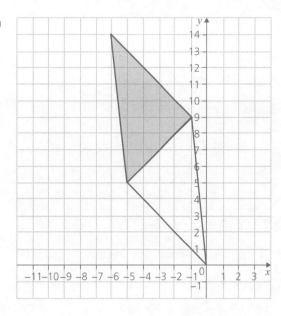

.................................................... [2]          .................................................... [2]

## Exercises 27.5–27.6

**1** In the following diagram, object A has been translated to each of the images B, C and D. Give the translation vector in each case.

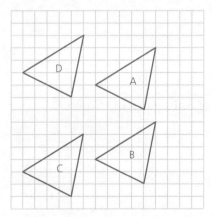

B = ............................................................ [1]

C = ............................................................ [1]

D = ............................................................ [1]

**2** In the diagram, translate the object by the vector $\begin{pmatrix} -2 \\ -4 \end{pmatrix}$.

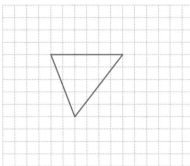

[2]

## Exercises 27.7–27.8

**1** Find the centre of enlargement and the scale factor of enlargement in these diagrams:

**a**

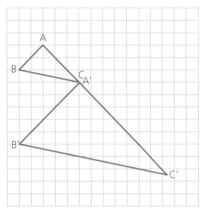

**b**

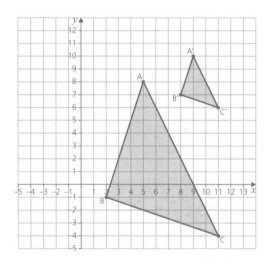

.................................................... [2]        .................................................... [2]

**2** Enlarge the object by the scale factor $\frac{1}{4}$ and from the centre of enlargement shown.

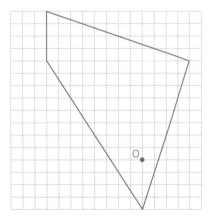

[2]

*Cambridge IGCSE® Core Mathematics Workbook*

# 28 Probability

## Exercises 28.1–28.4

1 Calculate the theoretical probability, when rolling an octahedral (8-sided and labelled 1–8), fair dice, of getting:

**a** a score of 6 ................................................................................................. [1]

**b** a score of 2 or 3 ......................................................................................... [1]

**c** an even number ......................................................................................... [1]

**d** a score of less than 1 ................................................................................. [1]

**e** a score of more than 1 ............................................................................... [1]

**f** a score of less than 4 or more than 4. ...................................................... [1]

2 23 girls and 17 boys enter a classroom in a random order. Calculate, giving your answer as a decimal, the probability that the first student to enter will be:

**a** a girl ..................................... [1]　　**b** a boy. ..................................... [1]

3 **a** Calculate the probability of being born in June. (Assume a non-leap year.)

.................................................................................................................. [1]

**b** Explain why the answer to **a** is not $\frac{1}{12}$ .

.................................................................................................................. [1]

**c** What is the probability of not being born in June?

.................................................................................................................. [1]

4 A computer uses the letters A, T or R at random to make three-letter words. Assuming a letter can be repeated, calculate the probability of getting:

**a** the letters R, R, R

.................................................................................................................. [3]

**b** any one of the words TAR, RAT or ART.

.................................................................................................................. [3]

**5** A container has 749 white sweets and 1 red sweet. Sweets are picked from the container one at a time and are not replaced. What is the probability of getting the red sweet if you pick:

**a** 1 sweet

**b** 500 sweets

.......................................[1]

.......................................[1]

**c** 150 sweets

**d** 750 sweets?

.......................................[1]

.......................................[1]

**6** The gender and age of members of a film club are recorded and shown in the table:

|  | Child | Adult | Senior |
|---|---|---|---|
| Male | 14 | 58 | 21 |
| Female | 18 | 44 | 45 |

**a** How many members has the film club? ........................................ [1]

**b** A member is picked at random. Calculate, giving your answer as a percentage, the probability that the member is:

**i** a child ........................................ [1]

**ii** female ........................................ [1]

**iii** a female child. ........................................ [1]

**7** A fair cubic dice and a fair tetrahedral (four faces) dice are rolled.

*Draw a two-way table on paper if necessary to help you.*

**a** Find the probability that both dice show the same number.

........................................ [3]

**b** Find the probability that the number on one dice is double the number on the other dice.

........................................ [2]

**8** Two fair octahedral dice are rolled. Find the probability of getting:

*Draw a table on paper if necessary to help you.*

**a** any double

........................................ [2]

**b** a total score of 13

............................................................................................................................. [2]

**c** a total score of 17

............................................................................................................................. [2]

**d** a total which is a multiple of 2, 3 or 5.

............................................................................................................................. [4]

## Exercise 28.5

**1** A football team plays three matches. In each match the team is equally likely to win, lose or draw.

  **a** Calculate the probability that the team:

    **i** wins no matches

    ............................................................................................................... [3]

    **ii** loses at least two matches.

    ............................................................................................................... [3]

  **b** Explain why it is not very realistic to assume that the outcomes are equally likely in this case of football matches.

  ............................................................................................................... [1]

**2** A spinner is split into fifths, numbered 1–5. If it is spun twice, calculate the probability of getting:

  **a** two fives

  ............................................................................................................... [2]

  **b** two numbers the same.

  ............................................................................................................... [3]

## Exercises 28.6–28.7

**1** A board game involves players rolling an octahedral dice. However, before a player can start, they need to roll an odd number. Calculate the probability of:

*Draw a tree diagram on paper if necessary to help you.*

  **a** getting an eight on the first throw ................................................................... [2]

  **b** starting within the first two throws ................................................................. [3]

  **c** not starting within the first three throws ....................................................... [3]

**d** starting within the first three throws. ............................................................ [3]

**e** If you add the answers to **c** and **d** what do you notice? Explain this result.

........................................................................................................................

........................................................................................................................ [2]

2 In England 40% of trucks are made abroad. Calculate the following probabilities:

**a** The next two trucks to pass a particular spot are both made in England.

........................................................................................................................ [3]

**b** Two of the next three trucks are made abroad.

........................................................................................................................ [3]

**c** Two or more of the next three trucks are made in England.

........................................................................................................................ [3]

3 A sweet tin contains 20 mints (M) and 80 toffees (T). A girl takes two sweets from the tin to eat.

**a** Complete the tree diagram below.

[3]

**b** Calculate the probability that the girl:

**i** doesn't pick any toffees

........................................................................................................................ [2]

**ii** picks one of each type of sweet?

........................................................................................................................ [2]

## Exercise 28.8

A photographer organises his photographs and realises that they are mainly of landscapes (L), buildings (B) or both. The Venn diagram summarises the number of each type of photograph.

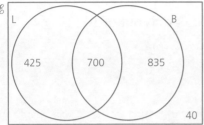

**a** Calculate the total number of photographs. ............................................................. [1]

**b** A photograph is selected at random. Calculate the probability that:

**i** it has no buildings .................................................................................... [1]

**ii** it has a landscape or buildings ..................................................................... [2]

**iii** it has a landscape or a building, but not both. .................................................. [2]

## Exercises 28.9–28.10

**1** To test whether a coin is biased Paolo spins it 10 times. It lands on heads 5 times. Anita spins the same coin 1000 times and finds it lands on heads 108 times.

Comment on whether you think the coin is likely to be biased or not, giving a reason for your answer.

.............................................................................................................................

............................................................................................................................. [2]

**2** Two friends are standing in a crowd of people. A person is picked at random from the crowd. How many people are in the crowd if the probability of either friend being picked is 0.004?

............................................................................................................................. [2]

# 29 Mean, median, mode and range

## Exercises 29.1–29.3

1 A student looks at the results of her last ten maths tests. Each score is out of 10.

   6  4  9  8  8  3  4  5  8  6

   Calculate:

   **a** the mean test score ................................................................................................. [1]

   **b** the median test score ............................................................................................... [1]

   **c** the modal test score ................................................................................................ [1]

   **d** the test score range. ................................................................................................ [1]

2 The mean mass of 15 rugby players in a team is 115.3 kg. The mean mass of the team plus a substitute is 114 kg. Calculate the mass of the substitute.

   ............................................................................................................................................ [2]

3 A chocolate manufacturer sells boxes with assorted chocolates. A number of the boxes are sampled and the number of chocolates inside recorded. The results are shown in the table.

   | Number of chocolates | 42 | 43 | 44 | 45 | 46 | 47 | 48 |
   |---|---|---|---|---|---|---|---|
   | Frequency | 3 | 7 | 8 | 7 | 9 | 5 | 1 |

   **a** How many boxes were sampled? ............................................................................... [1]

   **b** What is the modal number of chocolates? ............................................................... [1]

   **c** Calculate the mean number of chocolates. .............................................................. [2]

   **d** Calculate the median number of chocolates. ........................................................... [1]

   **e** Calculate the range of the number of chocolates. ................................................... [1]

4 Eight people are weighed. Their masses (kg) are as follows:

   75        $x$        92        46        71        84        $y$        97

   Two masses are unknown and are given as $x$ and $y$. The mean of the eight masses is 74 kg, the median 73 kg and the range 51 kg. Calculate a possible pair of values for $x$ and $y$.

   ............................................................................................................................................

   ............................................................................................................................................ [3]

*Cambridge IGCSE® Core Mathematics Workbook*

# 30 Collecting, displaying and interpreting data

## Exercises 30.1–30.4

**1** The ages of people who saw two different films are shown in the comparative bar chart below.

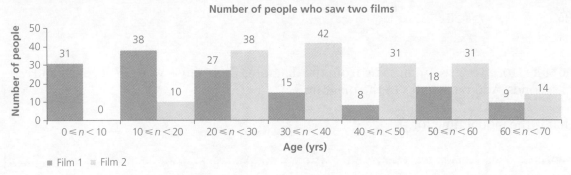

**Number of people who saw two films**

■ Film 1  ■ Film 2

**a  i** One film was for an adult audience. Which one of the two films was it?

..........................................................................................................................................................[1]

**ii** Justify your answer to **i**.

..........................................................................................................................................................[1]

**b** How many people watched film 1?

..........................................................................................................................................................[2]

**c** How many people in the age range $30 \leqslant n < 50$ watched film 2?

..........................................................................................................................................................[1]

**2** The time taken for girls and boys at a sports club to run 300 m, in seconds, is given in the back-to-back stem and leaf diagram below.

```
Girls          Boys
          5 | 3
9 5 5  | 6 | 1 2
   2 1 | 7 | 4 6 8 9
   8 6 | 8 | 1 4 8 9
 4 1 0 | 9 | 2 3 3
   4 0 |10 | 2        Key    3|8|2 is 83 seconds for a girl and
       1|11|                 82 seconds for a boy
```

**a** The times for two girls are missing from the diagram. Their times were 97 seconds and 115 seconds. Add their times to the diagram. [1]

**b** What is the modal time for:

 **i** girls ................................................................................................................[1]

 **ii** boys? ...............................................................................................................[1]

**c** Calculate the median time for:

 **i** girls ................................................................................................................[1]

 **ii** boys. ...............................................................................................................[1]

**d** Which of the averages calculated in **b** and **c** gives a better summary of the results? Justify your answer.

 ...............................................................................................................................

 ..........................................................................................................................[2]

**3** In 2016, the Olympics were held in Rio de Janeiro. 15 athletes were chosen at random and their height (cm) and mass (kg) were recorded. The results are shown below.

| Height/cm | Mass/kg | Height/cm | Mass/kg |
|---|---|---|---|
| 201 | 120 | 166 | 65 |
| 203 | 93 | 160 | 41 |
| 191 | 97 | 189 | 82 |
| 163 | 50 | 198 | 106 |
| 166 | 63 | 204 | 142 |
| 183 | 90 | 179 | 88 |
| 182 | 76 | 154 | 53 |
| 183 | 87 | | |

**a** What type of correlation (if any) would you expect between a person's height and mass? Justify your answer.

..................................................................................................................................................................

.......................................................................................................................................................... [2]

**b** Plot a scatter graph on the grid below. Two of the points have been plotted for you.

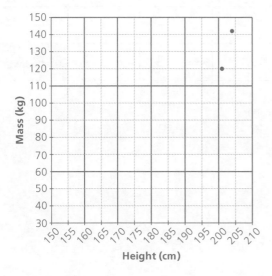

Height (cm)

[3]

**c i** Calculate the mean height of the athletes. ..................................................................... [1]

**ii** Calculate the mean mass of the athletes. ..................................................................... [1]

**iii** Plot the point representing the mean height and mean mass of the athletes. Label it M. [1]

**d** Draw a line of best fit for the data that passes through the mean point M. ..................... [1]

**e i** From the results you have plotted, describe the correlation between the height and mass of the athletes.

.......................................................................................................................................................... [1]

**ii** How does the correlation compare with your prediction in **a**?

.......................................................................................................................................................... [1]

4 The ages of people, selected randomly, travelling on an aeroplane are given in the grouped frequency table:

| Age (years) | 0– | 10– | 20– | 30– | 40– | 50– | 60– | 70–80 |
|---|---|---|---|---|---|---|---|---|
| Frequency | 10 | 18 | 23 | 60 | 50 | 75 | 35 | 10 |

Represent the information as a histogram on the grid. Two bars have been drawn for you.

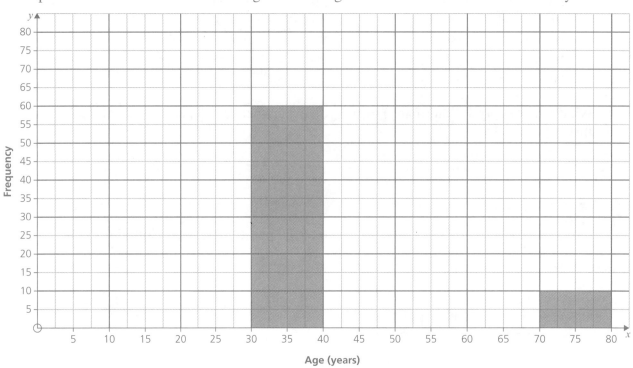

Age (years)

[3]

**5** Eight different cars are selected at random. Their mass (kg) is recorded, as is their average fuel consumption (km/l). The results are presented in the table below.

| Mass (kg) | 2150 | 1080 | 1390 | 1820 | 900 | 1210 | 1620 | 810 |
|---|---|---|---|---|---|---|---|---|
| Average fuel consumption (km/l) | 5.1 | 11.2 | 7.8 | 6.5 | 15.1 | 10.7 | 11.6 | 12.0 |

**a** Plot a scatter graph on the grid below.

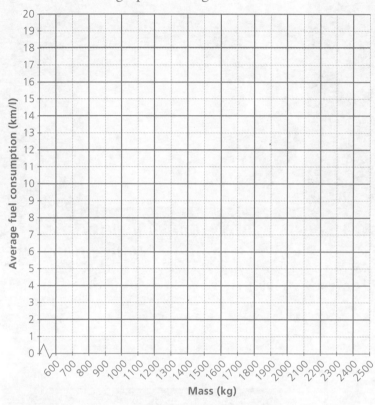

[3]

**b** Describe the correlation between mass and fuel consumption.

.................................................................................................................................................

....................................................................................................................................... [2]

**c** Draw a line of best fit on your graph by eye. [1]

**d** Another car has a mass of 1500 kg. Use your line of best fit to estimate its likely average fuel consumption.

....................................................................................................................................... [1]

**e** Another car has a fuel consumption of 6 km/l. Use your line of best fit to estimate its likely mass.

....................................................................................................................................... [1]

**f** A car manufacturer is thinking of producing a car of mass 500 kg and states that it will have a fuel consumption of 15 km/l. Comment on the validity of this statement.

.................................................................................................................................................

....................................................................................................................................... [2]

Reinforce learning and deepen understanding of the key concepts covered in the revised syllabus; an ideal course companion or homework book for use throughout the course.

» Develop and strengthen skills and knowledge with a wealth of additional exercises that perfectly supplement the Student's Book.

» Build confidence with extra practice for each lesson to ensure that a topic is thoroughly understood before moving on.

» Ensure students know what to expect with hundreds of rigorous practice and exam-style questions.

» Keep track of students' work with ready-to-go write-in exercises.

» Save time with all answers available online in the Online Teacher's Guide.

**Use with *Cambridge IGCSE® Core Mathematics* 4th edition**
9781510421660

For over 25 years we have been trusted by Cambridge schools around the world to provide quality support for teaching and learning. For this reason we have been selected by Cambridge Assessment International Education as an official publisher of endorsed material for their syllabuses.

Working for over
**25 YEARS**
WITH
Cambridge Assessment International Education

This resource is endorsed by
Cambridge Assessment International Education

✓ Provides learner support for the Core content of the Cambridge IGCSE® and IGCSE® (9–1) Mathematics syllabuses (0580/0980) for examination from 2020

✓ Has passed Cambridge International's rigorous quality-assurance process

✓ Developed by subject experts

✓ For Cambridge schools worldwide

**HODDER EDUCATION**
www.hoddereducation.com